THE
Agatha Christie
MISCELLANY

THE
Agatha Christie
MISCELLANY

CATHY COOK

First published 2013

The History Press
The Mill, Brimscombe Port
Stroud, Gloucestershire, GL5 2QG
www.thehistorypress.co.uk

British Library Cataloguing in Publication Data.
A catalogue record for this book is available from the British Library.

ISBN 978 0 7524 7960 6

Typesetting and origination by The History Press
Printed in Great Britain

· CONTENTS ·

To Bobby Cook

· ACKNOWLEDGEMENTS ·

SPECIAL THANKS GO TO my wonderful husband for bearing with me while I've been distracted writing this book, for encouraging me to write the Christie Mystery website in the first place, and for loving me as much as I love him – completely.

To Kim for being the best friend ever and being so enthusiastic and supportive about the book; to Jackie and Karen for convincing me to write the book in the first place; to Zowie for providing some excellent illustrations, to Rhoda who is a wonderful assistant and friend, and who has kept work distractions to a minimum whilst I persevered with the writing.

Also to the best parents anyone could ask for, Norman and Chris Luzmore, and my two elder brothers Peter and Ian whom I completely adore, even though we all know that I am really Mum's favourite!

And finally to Mark Beynon, my editor, who on the basis of my website trusted me enough that I would have the enthusiasm and dedication to get this book finished – thank you for your belief in me.

10 THINGS YOU MIGHT NOT KNOW ABOUT AGATHA CHRISTIE

'If anyone writes about my life in the future, I'd rather they got the facts right'.

Agatha Christie – *The Sunday Times* 27 February 1966

1. Agatha Christie was half American. Her American father, Frederick Miller, was able to trace his descendants from an old New England family. However, he died when she was only 11.

2. Agatha Christie never went to school. She was educated at home by her mother.

3. Agatha Christie had to wait five years before her first book was accepted for publication.

4. The Orient Express was nearly the death of Agatha Christie. Shortly before writing her famous book, *Murder on the Orient Express*, she slipped on an icy platform and fell underneath the stationary train in Calais. A railway porter quickly pulled her off the rails just before the train started moving.

5. Agatha Christie said that she did her best thinking while lying in the bath, eating apples and drinking cups of tea. She claimed that modern baths weren't made with authors in mind as they were too slippery, with no nice wooden ledge to rest pencils and paper on.

6. Agatha Christie worked as a nurse during the First World War, and once said that if she hadn't been a detective story writer, she would have quite liked to have been a hospital nurse.

7. Both Agatha Christie and her second husband, Max Mallowan, lied about their ages when they were married, to minimise the fourteen-year age gap. On their marriage certificate, Agatha's age is shown as 37 (when she was really 40), and Max is shown as 31 (when he was only 26).

8. Although a fictional character, Agatha Christie claimed to have seen the personification of Hercule Poirot twice in real life. Once while lunching in the Savoy grill room she saw Poirot just across at the next table, an exact replica in

every way, and another time she saw him on a boat going to the Canary Islands. She was too shy to approach either man.

9. Married to archaeologist Max Mallowan, Agatha Christie denied ever saying, 'An archaeologist is the best husband a woman can have. The older she gets the more interested he is in her.' Indeed, in an interview with Sir Francis Wyndham in the London *Sunday Times*, she said that she would have liked to have wrung the neck of the person who ever suggested that she had said it!

10. Agatha Christie predicted 'once I've been dead 10 years I'm sure nobody will ever have heard of me'. She died in 1976…

1

HER MYSTERIES & HOW TO SOLVE THEM

There exists a miscellany of trivia about the novels of Agatha Christie, her characters and her methods of murder. With fifty-seven years' worth of novels to choose from, this section will guide you through some of the more bizarre and interesting. It also includes advice on the rooms to stay out of if you ever find yourself in the middle of an Agatha Christie murder mystery!

• The Strangest Character to Appear in an Agatha Christie Novel •

In the early 1940s, during the Second World War, Agatha Christie wrote the two final novels for her most famous detectives, Hercule Poirot (*Curtain: Poirot's Last Case*) and Miss Marple (*Sleeping Murder*), just in case she did not survive the wartime bombing raids.

However, in *Sleeping Murder*, which was published post-humously in 1976, there appears a character which also appeared in her 1968 Tommy and Tuppence novel, *By the Pricking of My Thumbs*.

She was unnamed in *Sleeping Murder*, but was a white-haired 'charming-looking old lady, who came into the room holding a glass of milk.' The old lady, who lived in a sanatorium and rest home in Norfolk, asked, 'Is it your poor child, my dear?' Then she said, 'Half past ten – that's the time. It's always at half past ten. Most remarkable.' And she concludes, 'Behind the fireplace. But don't say I told you.'

In *By the Pricking of My Thumbs*, Tuppence meets an old lady with white hair who was holding a glass of milk in her hand. The old lady was called Mrs Julia Lancaster and lived in a nursing home. She asks, 'Excuse me, was it your poor child?' 'That's where it is, you know. Behind the fireplace', and, 'Always the same time of day … Ten past eleven. Yes, it's always the same time every morning'.

In both novels, the mystery of the old lady, the child, the fireplace and the time remains unsolved. Yet it is undoubtedly the same character, appearing in two stories that were written with twenty years between them. Who was she and why does she appear? We will never know.

•The Character with the Biggest Coincidence •

Agatha's second husband Max tells of a letter that they received from Mary Ann Zerkowski, the headmistress of a school in Pennsylvania, USA in 1970. She wrote that she had just finished reading Agatha's novel *Passenger to Frankfurt*, and was astonished to find herself playing the part of an undercover agent!

Mary Ann Zerkowski was really thrilled to be cast in the role, but was curious as to how Agatha had christened the spy with her name. She wrote that the book had created quite a sensation in her home town, and she was receiving many telephone calls and letters from friends addressing her as Countess Zerkowski.

Agatha wrote back that the name Zerkowski had been picked by pure chance, probably from the birth, death or marriage column in a newspaper, or from a telephone directory. However, she ended by congratulating the lady on having become a countess!

• Characters Based on Real-Life People •

In an interview with Lord Snowdon in the last years of her life, Agatha Christie said that she had become tired of being repeatedly asked if she took her characters from real life. She was adamant throughout her career that she invented them; that she had to, otherwise they didn't become real for her. She needed them to do what she wanted them to do, be what she wanted them to be, and think what she wanted them to think – so becoming alive for her.

In writing her first novel, Agatha Christie looked around for inspiration for her characters. She initially started to base her murderer on an acquaintance who lived nearby, but even though she considered it at some length, she could not see the man in question ever murdering anyone. Agatha, therefore, decided once and for all not to use real people as inspiration; she would create her characters for herself. She started looking out for people in trams, trains and restaurants which she could use as her starting point, and this worked well.

Agatha Christie tried again later on in her writing career to incorporate a close friend, Major Belcher, into one of her stories. They had gone on a round-the-world trip together in 1922 and, on their return, Belcher had badgered her to make him the murderer in the book she was writing, *The Man in the Brown Suit*. She found this incredibly difficult, and it was only when she gave the character a completely different name that the character really started to develop, even though he did use some of Belcher's phrases and anecdotes.

There is little doubt however that certain people she met influenced her development of certain characters. The masterful wife of an eminent archaeologist that Max Mallowan and Agatha worked with on a dig in Ur, Katharine Woolley, featured prominently in the character of Mrs Louise Leidner in *Murder in Mesopotamia* (1936). Max commented that Agatha became quite apprehensive that she had maybe gone a bit too close to the bone in her description of the tyrannical woman. However, Katharine Woolley appeared not to have recognised certain characteristic traits which might have been taken as descriptive of her. She saw no comparison and therefore was not offended. Agatha had however learnt her lesson and did not mirror people she had met quite so closely in future. In *Murder in Mesopotamia*, Max also featured as a minor character, David Emmott, who was a thoroughly decent chap!

Agatha Christie gave some insight into her choice of character names when she discussed it with the author Ernest Dudley. She explained how certain names conjured certain images of people in her mind. So for example, she saw a character called Raymond as a very blond man, whereas Dudley saw Raymond as slimish, dark and almost foreign looking.

In 1956, a French millionaire M. Nicoletis threatened legal proceedings against Agatha Christie. He claimed that her character Mrs Nicoletis, the owner of a student hostel in *Hickory Dickory Dock*, was based on his mother who had also owned a hostel where Agatha and her mother had once stayed. Agatha responded to her agent saying that she had invented the name Nicoletis, and it was terrible to invent a character which turns out to be so true to life.

Agatha often gave her characters unusual names that would take a bit of getting used to for the reader, so that in time the character became firmly entrenched in the reader's mind.

• WHEN IT ALL GOES WRONG •

In *Death in the Clouds* (1935), set on an aeroplane, the murder was committed using a lethal dose of snake venom on the end of a thorn, which was shot from a South American Indian blowpipe. However, many expert fans wrote in to complain that such blowpipes were far too long to hide in an aeroplane seat. With self-deprecating humility, in *Mrs McGinty's Dead* (1952), Agatha allowed her character Ariadne Oliver to narrate, with chagrin, the error of using the inappropriate blow pipe in one of her own detective stories.

INCONSISTENCIES IN HER STORIES

Colonel Arthur Bantry, the owner of Gossington Hall in St Mary Mead appeared first in *The Body in the Library* (1942). By the time of *The Mirror Crack'd from Side to Side* (1962), Colonel Bantry had died and his wife had sold Gossington Hall. However, he returns from the dead, alive and well, in Miss Marple's final case, *Sleeping Murder* (1976).

Miss Marple's nephew, Raymond West, is married to a lady who is introduced as Joyce in *The Thirteen Problems* (1932), but is called Joan in 'The Regatta Mystery' (1939).

Hercule Poirot moves from Kings Abbott after *The Murder of Roger Ackroyd* (1926) to live in Whitehaven Mansions in London, where he is residing at the time of *The ABC Murders* (1936). However, the name of the apartment block changes to Whitehouse

Florin Court, Charterhouse Square, London, was used by the producers of the *Poirot* TV series as the location of Poirot's apartment – he lived at Apartment 56B.

Mansions in *Cat Among the Pigeons* (1959) and is referred to as Whitefriars Mansions in *Elephants Can Remember* (1972).

In the novel *Postern of Fate* (1973), Tommy and Tuppence Beresford's daughter Deborah has twins early in the story, but towards the end she arrives at her parents' house with her three children aged 15, 11 and 7 – no twins.

In her autobiography, Agatha Christie commented on the mistake she made by creating the character of Hercule Poirot as already being in his 60s in the first book. Already retired and elderly when he first appears, he has to be about 120 years old by the time of his last appearance in *Curtain* (1975).

LIVE PERFORMANCE DISASTER 1

Agatha Christie described the first television broadcast of one of her books as something close to a farce. It was a black and white production of *And Then There Were None* in 1949, broadcast from the Alexandra Palace studios. At the time, productions could not be pre-recorded, so the programme went out live at 8.30 p.m. Early on in the production there was a huge crash to be heard off camera, shortly followed by the sound boom swinging into view over the actors' heads. After an uncertain start, the next half an hour was faultless, apart from one actor speaking his words into the wrong camera.

However, things then went downhill again with out of focus shots and a view of the camera crew wheeling equipment to a different part of the set. The thing that upset Agatha Christie most, making her 'livid', was that one of the actors, having been stabbed to death, got up and strolled away with his hands in his pockets, quite unaware that he was still in view.

LIVE PERFORMANCE DISASTER 2

One of Agatha Christie's plays, *Verdict*, was booed on its first night in 1956 because the assistant stage manager dropped the curtain down on the final scene about forty seconds too soon. This prevented the surprise re-entrance of a key character and two vital lines of dialogue, and so completely changed the ending of the play. Not realising that they had missed the ending, the audience and critics were very disappointed, saying the last scene 'rang false and fell flat'. The next night, with the right ending, the company took six curtain calls.

MGM's Miss Marple Films

In an interview for *The Sunday Times* in February 1966, Agatha Christie explained that she had always steered clear of films as she felt that they would cause her too many heartaches. Indeed, she had become so weary of stage adaptations of her books that did not stay true to the novels, that she had started to adapt them herself, rather than relying on others.

In 1960, in an attempt to extend her reading public, Agatha had agreed to sell the rights to MGM, with the provisional intention that MGM would use them as the basis of a television series. However, a sudden demand in America for British comedy films meant that they were made into movies starring Margaret Rutherford as Miss Marple. Agatha describes the whole experience as 'too awful', with poor climaxes, since you could tell exactly where the story was going. She said that she got immeasurable pleasure when they were not successful.

However, fans of Margaret Rutherford were delighted, and flocked to cinemas around the world. Reviewers were, on the whole, in favour of the films, and a whole new generation of fans started to read Agatha Christie books. Without doubt Margaret Rutherford was the first actress to create a lasting impression as Miss Marple with the general public, although

Rutherford never really wanted to take the role. Initially concerned about violence and murder, it took the film's director to convince her that she should play the part. It was also suggested that there would be a part for her real-life husband, the actor Stringer Davis, as Miss Marple's trusted assistant, the village librarian.

Four stories were brought to the screen starring Margaret Rutherford as Miss Marple, even though only one of the films was based on a Miss Marple book, with two books originally starring Hercule Poirot. MGM wrote their own script for the last film, *Murder Ahoy*, which was not actually based on any of Agatha's books. When Christie learned of the plan to

Browns Hotel, London, is alleged to be the inspiration for Bertram's Hotel, the setting for the Miss Marple novel *At Bertram's Hotel* (1965).

produce a wholly invented plot, she objected most strongly. In 1964 she wrote to MGM saying that she could not see how they could expect her 'to feel anything but deep resentment at your high-handed action', and felt it highly 'questionable that you have the right to act as you have done'. To have her characters incorporated into someone else's film was 'monstrous and highly unethical'. MGM ignored her objections, and carried on anyway. On its release, Agatha Christie described it as one of the silliest things she had ever seen, saying that she was delighted to note that it got some very bad reviews.

Rather unfortunately, one reviewer remarked that Margaret Rutherford was outfitted in a 'regular tarpaulin of a sweater', which created the effect of a 'warmly bundled English bulldog'. The reviewer was no doubt unaware that Rutherford wore her own clothes for the part of Miss Marple.

• REAL-LIFE CRIMES AND THE WORK OF AGATHA CHRISTIE •

CASE 1 – SOLVED THANKS TO AGATHA CHRISTIE

1975, London – Agatha Christie's detective story *The Pale Horse* provided a vital clue and saved a 19-month-old girl from dying of a condition that had baffled London doctors. According to the *British Journal of Hospital Medicine*, a trainee Canadian nurse in her 20s, Marsha Maitland, was off duty reading *The Pale Horse*. In it, one of the victims is poisoned with thallium and the nurse noticed that the symptoms closely resembled those of the baby. Thallium was rare in Britain, even though it had once been used to treat children for ringworm before its danger was realised. However, in the Middle East it was used as a household poison to kill rats and other vermin.

The 19-month-old girl had been brought to England from her home in Qatar in the Middle East, suffering from a mystery disease. Harley Street's specialists had been unable to diagnose her illness. She had shown all the same symptoms of the murder victims in the Christie thriller, but it was the girl's hair falling out that prompted Maitland to talk to the doctors. By this stage, the doctors felt that any suggestion was welcome. They approached Scotland Yard for help in testing for thallium poisoning and the police suggested they talk to a life-sentence prisoner called Graham Young, the Bovingdon Poisoner. He knew about thallium as he had kept detailed notes on the effects that it had as he poisoned his pet rabbits, his family and some of his co-workers.

However, the doctors didn't need to consult Young because their initial tests confirmed Nurse Maitland's suspicions – the child's body contained ten times the safe dose of the poison. The girl had ingested the poison over a long period as it was being used to kill cockroaches and rodents near her home. After three weeks of treatment, the baby left hospital, returning four months later for a check-up when she showed 'remarkable' improvement.

CASE 2 – MURDER INSPIRED BY AGATHA CHRISTIE

1977, Creances, France – Roland Roussell admitted to using a poison that he had read about in Agatha Christie's short story, 'The Tuesday Club Murder', to poison a bottle of red wine. Police found the book in Roussell's apartment in France, with the relevant passage on poisons underlined – the murderer uses atropine, a medicine to treat eye aliments, to kill his victim.

Roussell put atropine into a bottle of Cotes du Rhone wine during the summer, with the intention of killing a female friend of the family whom he believed was responsible for his mother's death. Roussell gave the bottle of wine to his uncle as a gift because the woman was a frequent visitor to his uncle's home, and she drank while his aunt and uncle abstained except during holidays.

However, his uncle saved the bottle of wine for the Christmas Eve dinner, and died within minutes of drinking the wine. His wife went into a coma and was rushed to hospital, and food poisoning was suspected. It wasn't until a few days later, when the village carpenter and the uncle's son-in-law each drank a glass of the wine that had been left on the dining table and lapsed into comas, that the link was made.

CASE 3 – PRISON WARDENS DISTRACTED BY AGATHA CHRISTIE

March 1959, Wormwood Scrubs prison, London – On Sunday, 15 March 1959, the West End cast of the Agatha Christie's play *The Mousetrap* arrived at London's notorious Wormwood Scrubs prison to give a special performance for the inmates. Three hundred prisoners watched the performance ... while two escaped. John Brian Meyers and David Dilwyn Gooding were reported missing. Both were serving three-year sentences – Meyers for shop breaking and Gooding for housebreaking.

CASE 4 – SERIAL KILLER 'INSPIRED' BY AGATHA CHRISTIE

May 2009, Qazvin, Iran – Mahin Qadiri, a 32-year-old woman, and Iran's first female serial killer, claimed that she was inspired by the novels of Agatha Christie. She told police that she drew tips on how to conceal her crimes from Christie's books, which had been translated into the language of Farsi.

Between February 2008 and May 2009, Mahin offered five elderly women a lift after prayers, then served them fruit juice laced with sedatives before strangling them and stealing their cash and jewellery.

CASE 5 – REAL-LIFE CRIME THAT INSPIRED AGATHA CHRISTIE TO WRITE *MURDER ON THE ORIENT EXPRESS*

The Lindbergh Baby – The motive behind the murder in *Murder on the Orient Express* (1934) focuses on the kidnapping of a child, Daisy Armstrong who was murdered after the ransom had been paid. Agatha Christie was inspired by a real-life kidnapping two years earlier.

In 1932 the 18-month-old son of famous American aviator, Charles Lindbergh, was kidnapped from his bedroom. A ransom note was left demanding $50,000 for his safe return. The ransom money was handed over a cemetery wall, as agreed, but the murdered baby was then found about 4 miles from where he had been taken. The US Congress rushed legislation to make kidnapping a federal crime.

The serial numbers on the banknotes were circulated to all banks in New York. However, it wasn't until two years later that one of the banknotes turned up at a petrol station, and luckily the attendant had written the man's car number plate in the margin because he had been acting suspiciously.

The evidence against German carpenter Bruno Richard Hauptmann was overwhelming: over $13,000 of the ransom money was found hidden in a can in his garage, handwriting experts suggested the writer of the ransom note was German, wood used to make the crude ladder employed in the kidnapping matched wood used as flooring in his attic, and the telephone number of the person who made the ransom-drop was found written on the door frame in the house.

CASE 6 – REAL-LIFE CRIME THAT INSPIRED AGATHA CHRISTIE TO WRITE *THE MOUSETRAP*

When Agatha Christie was asked by the BBC to write a radio play to commemorate Queen Mary's 80th birthday, she was inspired by a real-life crime that had horrified the nation. Dennis O'Neill was a 12-year-old boy, who with his younger brother, had been placed with foster parents at a remote farm in Minsterley, Shropshire. The two children were starved and abused by their foster parents, Reginald and Esther Gough, and the death of Dennis O'Neill led to a reform of foster caring in the UK, in particular the vetting of foster parents and regular visits to check on the foster children.

Agatha had kept a newspaper article of the case from the *Sunday Mirror*, and had written on the top that this had been her inspiration for *The Mousetrap*. A classic whodunit with an unexpected twist, *The Mousetrap* has been playing continuously in the West End since 1952.

• AGATHA CHRISTIE'S WORLD RECORDS •

Most translated author – According to UNESCO's inventory of book translations (the Index Translationum), Agatha Christie is the most translated author in history. To date there have been 6,598 translations of her novels, short stories and plays. Two of the more recent languages added include Maltese and Manx.

Longest theatrical run – *The Mousetrap* got its first Guinness World Record on 12 April 1958, when it became the longest-running play in the history of British theatre. It started at the Ambassador Theatre, in London's West End,

The Mousetrap has been playing in London since 1952, before Queen Elizabeth II came to the throne.

in 1952 and transferred to the adjacent St Martin's Theatre in London in 1974, where it has been playing ever since.

Thickest book published – it measures 322mm (12.67in) in width and contains all of Agatha Christie's Miss Marple stories in one volume. There are twelve novels and twenty short stories collected in one book, which was unveiled by HarperCollins in London on 20 May 2009.

• CHANGING THE NAMES FOR THE AMERICAN MARKET •

Quite often the names of Agatha Christie's books were changed for the American market. Sometimes there were obvious reasons, but at other times the reasons are less apparent, such as the change of the name of *The Sittaford Mystery* in the UK to *Murder at Hazelmoor* in America.

The American title of *Murder on the Orient Express* was changed to *Murder in the Calais Coach* to avoid confusion with Graham Greene's 1932 novel *Stanboul Train*, which was published in America as *Orient Express*.

The *4.50 from Paddington* was originally titled *4.54 from Paddington*, before Collins changed the title at the last minute. Interestingly, in the American version of the book which was entitled *What Mrs McGillicuddy Saw*, the train keeps its 4.54 departure time.

Finally, for understandable reasons, the original book title of *Ten Little Niggers* was renamed three times for both US and UK markets – *The Nursery Rhyme Murders, Ten Little Indians* and *And Then There Were None*.

Other books renamed for the American market include:

The Thirteen Problems	*The Tuesday Club Murders*
Lord Edgware Dies	*Thirteen at Dinner*
Why Didn't They Ask Evans?	*The Boomerang Clue*
Three Act Tragedy	*Murder in Three Acts*
Dumb Witness	*Poirot Loses a Client*
One, Two, Buckle My Shoe	*The Patriotic Murders*
Five Little Pigs	*Murder in Retrospect*
Sparkling Cyanide	*Remembered Death*
The Hollow	*Murder after Hours*
Taken at the Flood	*There is a Tide*
After the Funeral	*Funerals are Fatal*
Destination Unknown	*So Many Steps to Death*

• The Butler Did It! •

In only one of her novels does Agatha Christie have the butler as a murderer, and he is one of a number of people involved in a revenge killing.

In another novel, the murderer disguises himself as the butler to commit the murder and then fakes the butler's disappearance.

In another book, the butler does have a past history of murder as he allowed a previous employer to die in order to collect an inheritance, but he isn't actually the murderer in the novel and instead becomes a victim.

Other popular occupations that Agatha picked for her murderers include doctors, nurses, dentists and pharmacists, politicians, secretaries, actors, policemen, teachers and housewives.

• Methods of Murder •

For a woman who abhorred violence, Agatha Christie domesticated murder in a way that no other author had done before or since. However, she claimed that, as far as she was aware, she had never actually met a murderer.

Agatha rarely described the corpse, and said that she didn't think she could personally look at a really ghastly, mangled body. As Mark Campbell pointed out, her light genteel murder mysteries were all the more gripping because they were so bloodless. It wasn't the blood that was scary, it was the paranoia – anyone could have done it!

She confessed that she had little knowledge of the usual implements used for murder, such as pistols and revolvers, which is why she usually killed off her victims with poison or a blunt instrument.

According to her husband, Max Mallowan, Agatha used to take endless trouble over getting her facts right. She would consult professional authorities on police practice, on the law and on procedures in the courts. He said that it gave her great satisfaction when a solicitor wrote complaining of her ignorance about the law of inheritance. She was able to write back and demonstrate that the lawyer himself was outdated, that the law had been changed and that her statement was correct!

When it came to poisons and their antidotes however, she used her experience as a trained dispenser to great effect. She used poison in eighty-three stories, according to a 1978 research paper by Peter and John Gwilt. Nevertheless, she still checked out her facts when she needed to, writing to a specialist in 1967 about the impact of putting thalidomide in birthday cake icing – how long would it take to impact? How many grains would be needed?

Her use of poisons was so detailed and expert in her first novel, *The Mysterious Affair at Styles*, that she earned the ultimate accolade – a review by the *Pharmaceutical Journal*:

'This novel has the rare merit of being correctly written.'

The reviewer stated that they had to believe that the author must have had pharmaceutical training or had called in an expert.

Methods of poisoning include:

- A curry containing arsenic, even though arsenic has no taste (*4.50 from Paddington*)
- A pink gin poisoned with stropanthin, which made the victim's lips go blue as she clasped her chest and fought for breath ('Triangle at Rhodes' within *Murder in the Mews*)
- A coffee poisoned with taxine taken from the leaves or berries of the yew tree (*A Pocket Full of Rye*)
- A blow-dart dipped in the venom of the tree snake (*Death in the Clouds*)
- Phosphorus poisoning, which gives similar symptoms to liver disease and causes phosphorescent breath (*Dumb Witness*)
- Nicotine poisoning causing general paralysis and breathing problems (*Three-Act Murder*)

Cyanide, with its bitter almond smell, causes dizziness, convulsions, difficulty breathing, frothing at the mouth and eventually death. Cyanide is used in *A Pocket Full of Rye*, *Endless Night*, *The Moving Finger*, *And Then There Were None*, *Poirot Investigates* and of course, *Sparkling Cyanide* when it is mixed with champagne.

Strychnine, which was used as a rat poison for many hundreds of years, was used in *The Mysterious Mr Quin*, *The Mysterious Affair at Styles*, *Death on the Nile*, and *Passenger to Frankfurt*. As a poison, it causes violent convulsions and difficulty in swallowing.

Morphine was used by Agatha in a number of murders, causing impairment of mental and physical performance, the inability to concentrate, mood changes and apathy, and with an overdose, ultimate death. It was used in *Murder on the Links*, *Why Didn't They Ask Evans?*, *Sad Cypress*, *Taken at the Flood*, *Hickory Dickory Dock*, and *By the Pricking of My Thumbs*.

Heart medications, such as digitalin, were used in *Postern of Fate*, *Crooked House*, 'Problem at Sea' and *Appointment with Death*. An overdose can slow the pulse and increase the amount of blood pumped by the heart, with nausea, vomiting, and visual disturbance.

When Agatha Christie wasn't using poison as her method of death, she used many and varied objects and methods:

- A kitchen skewer thrust into the base of the skull (*The Moving Finger*)
- A ukulele string ('The Bird with the Broken Wing' in *The Mysterious Mr Quin*)
- A raincoat belt (*Three Blind Mice*)
- A dart from a blowgun (*Death in the Clouds*)
- A fireplace poker (*Ordeal by Innocence*)

- Nylon stockings (*A Pocket Full of Rye*)
- A golf club (*Spider's Web*)
- An electrified chessboard (*The Big Four*)
- A marble paperweight slipped into a woollen sock (*Hickory Dickory Dock*)
- An ancient grain millstone (*Murder in Mesopotamia*)

Murder by gunshot was used in amongst others novels: *One, Two, Buckle My Shoe*, *And Then There Were None*, *Peril at End House*, *Death on the Nile*, *At Betram's Hotel*, *The Unexpected Guest* and *Murder at the Vicarage*.

Murder by stabbing or sharp implement was used in *Death on the Nile*, *Murder on the Orient Express*, *Cards on the Table*, *Hercule Poirot's Christmas*, and *After the Funeral*.

• MOTIVES FOR MURDER •

Motives for murder are many and varied in Agatha Christie's books. However, money or protection is often the driving force. Over and over again, greed means that murderers seek to inherit by killing, and usually the victim has several potential heirs, providing a number of suspects.

Killing a blackmailer, or murder to ensure that a guilty secret is kept, are also common themes. The theme of sexual revenge, sexual passion and physical attractiveness is often important to her plot, featuring in fifteen of her fifty-four 'true' detective novels (as opposed to her thrillers) – many will murder or risk murder in order to secure the partner they desire.

However, Agatha Christie steers clear of the common causes of actual murder, namely domestic violence and drunken brawls.

It is interesting that, probably due to the strong female influence in her upbringing, there is not a single instance in Agatha Christie's books of a murder involving the killing of a mother by a daughter, or a daughter by a mother. Yet sons murder mothers and fathers, and fathers murder sons. However, she is very even-handed when it comes to choosing male and female murderers.

• Letting them Get Away with Murder •

In a large number of cases, Agatha Christie convinces us that there is a moral case for allowing the killer to get away with murder. She allows her murderers to die or commit suicide before they get brought to justice. In occasional circumstances she even allows them to get away completely with the crime.

Her novels were primarily occupied with good versus evil, and the supreme wrong of taking a life. They have been described as a modern version of the medieval morality plays, rather than being about justice and legality.

Some murderers are allowed to take their own lives, and exit gracefully, rather than be subjected to disgrace and the gallows, often with the support of Hercule Poirot himself.

So, for example, the killers in *The Murder of Roger Ackroyd* and *Peril at End House* are never brought to trial.

In other stories, Agatha allows her detective to decide that there were mitigating circumstances, or even that the murder was justified, and that some form of moral balance has been restored. In such circumstances, the murderer is allowed to walk away without any form of justice, such as in *Murder on the Orient Express*. In this novel, Hercule Poirot even goes so far as to decide to present a false scenario of the murder to the officials to protect the guilty.

Agatha Christie also allows members of the family to sort out the bad seed in their family and rid the world of a killer. In one of Agatha's short stories, Hercule Poirot allows a correctly motivated mother to poison her son and escape the law, after she sees her son murder his wife, and realises what sort of man she has brought into the world.

Similarly, in *The Mirror Crack'd from Side to Side*, Miss Marple allows the compassionate spouse of the murderer to put them to eternal sleep, rather than face trial. Justice is achieved.

• THE DETECTIVE STORY AS A PUZZLE-GAME •

In Patricia Maida and Nicholas Spornick's study of Agatha Christie's work, they state that at the heart of the detective story is the puzzle-game. There are components within the books that are common to all games – firstly there must a goal, and in the case of detective fiction, this is identifying the murderer or 'whodunit?'

The puzzle-game must have a playing board (the setting of the murder) and players (the murderer, the suspects and the detective). There must be rules for fair play (the conventions of the detective story writing genre, such as Ronald Knox's 10 Rules of Detective Fiction, as discussed below).

And finally, there must be devices used to reach the goal of the game (clues), as well as barriers and handicaps (red herrings and plot devices).

The reader who plays the game must have at least a fair chance of achieving the goal (solving the mystery).

• The 10 Rules of Detective Fiction – Ronald Knox & The Detection Club •

During the 1920s, 'rules' or conventions for the detective story as a genre were laid down by many writers, most notably by Father Ronald Knox. His 'Detective Decalogue' can be summarised as follows:

1. The criminal must be mentioned early on in the story
2. Supernatural solutions are not allowed
3. Only one secret room or passage should be permitted and should be mentioned earlier in the story if it is to assist with the solution
4. No undiscovered poisons or poisons unknown to science are permitted
5. No Chinamen should appear in the story (how bizarre!)

6. The detective must not be helped by either lucky accident or by intuition
7. The detective must not himself commit the crime
8. The detective must not conceal clues or misinform the reader
9. The thoughts of the detective's sidekick or 'Watson' must not be concealed
10. There must be special warning if twin brothers or doubles are to be used

***

Nowadays it seems strange that such rules would ever have been taken seriously, but at the time a great many writers worked carefully within them. The general principle was that the reader, although they can be surprised by the ending of the story, should be able to go back through and see the clues they missed.

In 1928, Dorothy L. Sayers and Anthony Berkeley dreamed up the idea of a unique and select club called the Detection Club. The club had strict rules as to who was eligible for membership, but all were detective writers, with G.K. Chesterton as the first president. Members swore to avoid 'Divine Revelation, Feminine Intuition, Mumbo-jumbo, Jiggery-pokery' and all other such dubious ploys in writing their detective stories.

Agatha Christie, renowned for her shyness and hatred of public speaking, only agreed to the presidency when Lord

Gorell said he would help her out by being co-president so that she would not have to make any speeches. She was president from 1958 until her death in 1976, and true to her word, she did not make a single speech during her eighteen years of office.

• PLOT DEVICES, RED HERRINGS AND CLUES •

CLUES AND RED HERRINGS

These were Agatha Christie's greatest plot device for misleading and confusing the reader. The key to solving the murder is to determine what is a real clue, and what is a worthless clue or red herring. Quite often the vital clues are given at the beginning of the book, but they are so underplayed that it is easy to miss them amongst all the other clues and red herrings that are presented.

Christie's red herrings are sometimes linked to unrelated minor crimes, which the reader is led to believe might be connected. Be wary though, because on occasions, everything really is as it seems.

THE LEAST LIKELY SUSPECT

It is vital for a good murder mystery story that the murderer approaches unnoticed, both to the victim and to the reader trying to solve the case. Quite often, it is the least likely suspect whom Agatha Christie has as her murderer. Often a watertight alibi leads the reader to believe that the suspect is completely innocent, only to have the alibi disproved at the last minute.

At other times, it is an individual whom you would expect to be completely above suspicion, such as a policeman or detective. In other crime novels, Agatha has the murderer being a child, the narrator and even all of the possible suspects.

Agatha Christie was accused of the unscrupulous use of the least-likely-person motive in *The Murder of Roger Ackroyd*, which caused a storm of discussion and outrage and she was accused of not playing fairly. Undeterred, she went on to produce a whole series of books, which played variations on the theme of the least likely suspect.

Unusually, Agatha Christie wrote a foreword for her book *Cards on the Table*. In it she took issue with the commonly held view that the murderer was always likely to be the least likely suspect, and explained that in her current novel, only four suspects would be presented, all with equal motive and an established track record as a murderer, so none could be regarded as the least likely.

THE DISGUISE

This plot device is frequently used in Agatha Christie's mystery stories; she uses both characters who alter their physical identity, and those who adopt a completely fake identity. The murderer would often pick an identity that was beyond suspicion, in order to set up the ultimate murder or to stalk their prey.

In some cases, a character disappears completely and then comes back in a different guise. In other crime stories, the murderer impersonates a long-lost family member to gain the trust of others. Characters sometimes feel that a suspect looks familiar, and Agatha uses this to indicate that the individual might be in disguise.

However, there is frequent debate about the credibility of such devices – sometimes a wig or a false beard, has everyone involved convinced that the character is someone completely different.

SERVANTS & DOMESTICS

In an era when many large houses still had a team of domestic staff to keep the place running, there were often servants in the background of Agatha Christie's stories, and they were useful plot devices.

These servants were usually seen and not heard, and therefore usually ignored. However, their evidence is often vital because they overhear and see things that others might not, simply because they melt into the background.

It is interesting to note that Christie's murderers were rarely from the domestic staff; unless of course the murderer was in disguise as a servant. Agatha did on occasion break the rules and have the murderer be a servant — after all, who better to commit the ultimate crime than someone who blends into the background?

THE BIG REVEAL

The most obvious and consistent plot device is that Agatha Christie doesn't reveal the whole truth until the end of the book, keeping the reader hooked and absorbed until the end. Until that final piece of the jigsaw is in place, the whole picture isn't revealed. There will undoubtedly be fake revelations along the way, causing you to believe that it's all over, but invariably there are a couple more chapters to go, so perhaps the whole truth hasn't properly been revealed yet.

• SOLVING HER MYSTERIES •

So are Agatha Christie's detective stories really solvable? It is certainly dangerous to expect any sort of equation to work consistently, but there are some things that can be borne in mind when reading her novels. Martin Fido, amongst others, identified a number of rules that are helpful in solving her mysteries. Here are my top 10:

1. If a person in the book has an excellent motive, but has been ruled out as a suspect because of lack of means or

opportunity, suspect that person. Don't forget they may have an accomplice, who they may pretend to hate.

2. A witness will on occasion reveal the name of the murderer or a vital clue early on in the novel, only for the witness to be discounted as unreliable, and so no one listens to them. Make sure you pay strict attention to even the most un-credible witness.

3. Ignore those questions that the detective says are important, as they are usually designed to mislead you into focusing on minor details that aren't crucial or relevant. Agatha Christie will use the conjuror's technique of directing your attention away from the real mechanism of the trick.

4. Look out for throwaway details in the lead up to the crime. Study carefully who was in the room, who slipped out for a few minutes, who was thought to be safely asleep somewhere else. Be suspicious of any tiny window of opportunity, however small, that is never mentioned again.

5. Always be on the lookout for disguise and impersonation. In the novels of Agatha Christie, a disguise can be so perfect that nobody recognises a person they have known all their lives, or to whom they were speaking just a few minutes earlier.

6. Agatha Christie quite often uses the word 'interesting' before a clue that is of little relevance, but then omits the word when writing about a clue which is vital to the plot.

7. The murderer may attempt to divert suspicion away from themselves by faking an attempt on their own life, or staging their own death, so appearing to be a victim. Attempted murders or actual murders can also be used by the suspect to mask the real murder. You can also be certain that the murderer will tell lies.

8. Remember that some names, like Chris and Hilary, can be given to either a man or woman, and all of the characters (including you) may be looking for a person of the wrong gender.

9. Rather bizarrely, as G.C. Ramsey points out, if an American actress figures prominently in the novel, scrutinise her movements and motives carefully.

10. Beyond that, as Dorothy Sayers once commented, 'It is the reader's business to suspect *everybody*'.

• MOST DANGEROUS ROOMS •

The most dangerous place to be in an Agatha Christie novel is the bedroom. A room of privacy and solitude, it proves the ideal place for the victim to be killed when they are least expecting it, usually asleep. Victims killed in their bedrooms can be found in *The Moving Finger*, *Crooked House*, *Hercule Poirot's Christmas*, *Sad Cypress*, *Cat Among the Pigeons*, *After the Funeral*, and the list goes on and on.

The Library – it is readily accessible and always open for anyone wishing to get a book, yet libraries in houses tend to be solitary places, not as social or busy as the Drawing Room where a murderer is likely to be interrupted. The book-lined shelves help muffle the screams of the dying. Victims killed in the library include those in *The Body in the Library* and *Pocket Full of Rye*.

The Study – again usually a solitary place, is full of items and ornaments which will retain the fingerprints of a care-less murderer. The heavy fireplace equipment can be used as a murder weapon, and the fireplace can be used to burn incriminating letters and other clues. The French windows facilitate the secret entry and exit of the murderer. The vic-tims in *Lord Edgware Dies* and *The Murder of Roger Ackroyd* are amongst those killed in their study.

The safest place in the house is the Kitchen – murders are never committed in the kitchen. The cook, usually large and experienced but extremely sensitive, is a comfort to the family, and nothing must be allowed to upset the cook in Agatha Christie's world!

However, even outside you might not be safe. You can be killed on the lawn (*Peril at End House*), near the swimming pool (*The Hollow*), on the cliffs (*Elephants Can Remember*) and in the boathouse (*Dead Man's Folly*).

• FAMOUS PEOPLE LINKED WITH AGATHA CHRISTIE •

Basil Rathbone, most famous for his portrayal of Sherlock Holmes, played a sinister fortune hunter intent on murdering rich women, in a 1937 film adaptation of Agatha Christie's play *Love From a Stranger*. In 1936, he recalled that this film was the picture that Darryl Zanuck saw before he cast Rathbone in the first of the Sherlock Holmes films, *The Hound of the Baskervilles*. So Basil Rathbone said that it was actually Agatha Christie who got him typecast as Holmes for all those years!

Appearing alongside Basil Rathbone in *Love From a Stranger*, was a young Joan Hickson. After seeing Joan Hickson play a small role in the play *Appointment with Death* in 1946, Agatha wrote to her saying:

I will call you to play my Miss Marple one day if I can find time to write another play – too many domestic chores.

Long after Agatha Christie's death, Joan Hickson was to play Miss Marple in the BBC's television series from 1984 until 1992.

Many household names made their earliest appearances in her plays – Harold Pinter, for example, appeared in several, such as *Murder at the Vicarage* at Whitby Spa Rep, and *Ten Little Indians* in Huddersfield Rep, both in 1954.

Miss Marple appeared on television before Hercule Poirot when, on 30 December 1956, a somewhat unconvincing Gracie Fields played the character in *A Murder is Announced* on NBC in America. The play was broadcast live from New York. One of the characters, Patrick Simmons, was played by a young man called Roger Moore, later to become James Bond.

Christopher Lee, famous as Count Dracula, was heard but not seen as the uncredited voice of the mysterious host, Mr U.N. Owen, in the film *Ten Little Indians* (1965).

When BBC Radio produced the first British serialisation of an Agatha Christie book in 1953, *Partners in Crime*, Richard Attenborough and his wife Sheila Sim (daughter of Alastair Sim) starred as Tommy and Tuppence Beresford. The previous November they had been the starring roles in the opening in London of *The Mousetrap*.

Agatha's novel *Peril at End House* was made into a successful stage version by Arnold Ridley. Famous for his role as the weak-bladdered Private Godfrey in *Dad's Army*, Ridley was actually a major playwright. His huge success was with *The Ghost Train* in 1923, and the royalties from this enabled him to live comfortably throughout his life, until his face became famous in the 1970s as Godfrey.

Agatha's last final public appearance in 1974 was to the London premiere of the film version of *Murder on the Orient Express*, where she was accompanied by Lord Louis Mountbatten. Mountbatten had been instrumental in getting Agatha to consent to allow his son-in-law to make the book into a film. She had been extremely reticent to ever allow another movie version of her books after the debacle of MGM's Margaret Rutherford Miss Marple films.

Lord Mountbatten had also been one of two people who had suggested, way back at the beginning of Agatha's career, that she might consider writing a book where the narrator was the murderer. This suggestion led to one of Agatha's most famous and talked about books of all time, and the controversy that surrounded whether she had 'played fair' went on for many years.

• FAMOUS FANS OF AGATHA CHRISTIE •

Gracie Fields was a huge fan of Agatha Christie and she had an almost complete collection of her books in the library of her home in Capri.

Former Prime Minister Clement Attlee said he admired and delighted in Agatha Christie's ingenuity and her capacity to keep a secret until she was ready to divulge it.

Sigmund Freud was a great lover of detective stories and Agatha Christie was one of his particular favourites.

The actor Donald Sutherland, who appeared in the film version of *Ordeal by Innocence*, said during filming that he had always loved whodunits. For a long time however he had never read any Agatha Christie, until he found himself stuck in a friend's house in France with nothing to read except a couple of Christie books. After being unable to put the first one down, he immediately read the second one and then went out to the local store, where he found another ten or so of her books. He bought them all and for a while always had one of them in his pocket.

The famous Angus McBean portrait of Agatha Christie. *Angus McBean Photograph (MS Thr 581).* © *Harvard Theatre Collection, Houghton Library, Harvard University.*

Queen Mary, the Queen's grandmother, was an enthusiastic fan of Agatha Christie and had a standing order with her bookseller so that she got every new book when it was published. When the BBC asked Queen Mary how she would like them to celebrate her 80th birthday in 1946, she requested an Agatha Christie play for the radio. And so *The Mousetrap* was born.

In fact, the admiration of Agatha Christie ran throughout the royal family: Queen Elizabeth the Queen Mother, Princess Margaret, and the current Queen Elizabeth II were all Agatha Christie fans. Indeed, when the Duke and Duchess of Windsor returned to London following Edward VIII's abdication from the throne to marry Wallis Simpson in the 1930s, Agatha Christie's *Witness for the Prosecution* was the first play they chose to see.

2

THE REAL AGATHA CHRISTIE

It has been said that it was impossible to meet Agatha Christie without instantly liking her. She has also been described as everyone's favourite aunt.

Her shyness, coupled with her intense yearning for privacy, meant that she was never totally at ease when attending public functions. She would rather sit and quietly observe people, than be the centre of attention.

She was without doubt a well-bred English lady. Peter Saunders, the producer of her plays, paid tribute to her after her death as being:

As English as Buckingham Palace, the House of Commons and the Tower of London.

One of the earliest recollections of Agatha Christie, or Agatha Miller as she was then, came from Joan Millyard who knew her as a girl in Devon. She describes Agatha as always fun and very bright. With her Scandinavian colouring and lovely complexion, she was a very pretty girl and several of the boys found her exceedingly attractive. However, there was also a quiet shyness about her.

Barbara Mullen was the first actress ever to play Miss Marple in the 1949 play of *Murder at the Vicarage*. She met Agatha Christie during the production and described her as a very reticent lady, very shy, 'who talked very little about herself'. However, she was also an acute observer, who just liked to watch all the time. Barbara says that they got on very well together, but Agatha didn't try to tell her how to play the part of Miss Marple, even though it was clear that she had her own ideas. She allowed Barbara to play the part as she wished.

Another famous Miss Marple actress, Joan Hickson, first performed in an Agatha Christie play in the 1940s. Joan Hickson played Miss Pryce in the 1945 play of *Appointment with Death*, and she remembers Agatha as 'absolutely charming, but also very shy'. Agatha went on tour with the production, but she did not talk very much. She did however have an uncanny knowledge of people. Joan also talks about Agatha's generosity and kindness, sharing her tea at a time when it was still rationed.

Sir Richard Attenborough and his wife Sheila Sim were the first to play starring roles in the play, *The Mousetrap*, and also starred in the first British radio serialisation of an Agatha Christie book, *Partners in Crime*, in 1953. Sir Richard Attenborough said of Agatha that she was the calmest and gentlest character that he had ever met and, as they got to know her over the years, they found her 'frankly incredible'. To look at her she resembled everyone's favourite aunt, but she knew her own mind, and put them right when they made mistakes. He says that she was 'a stickler for things being absolutely right'. His wife, Sheila Sim, described Agatha as 'such a gentle, unassuming lady' – 'the most unlikely person to have written all those murder stories'.

Of course the person who knew Agatha Christie best was her second husband, Max Mallowan, who was married to her for forty-five years. In his memoirs he describes her as woman of high intelligence and integrity, but who never claimed to be an intellectual. He says that she was a woman without ambition who could have shone in many areas if she had so chosen. He also comments on her elusiveness:

A defensive resistance to inquisitive probing, an in-built armour off which any questionnaire was liable to glance like a spent arrow.

In keeping with this desperate desire for privacy, there is remarkably little within his memoirs about the true character of Agatha Christie.

A common theme amongst those who met Agatha Christie was the way she would quietly sit and observe. The daughter of the local vicar at Ashfield remembers regular visits from Agatha to the vicarage, but she always felt that Agatha was observing her for a future character in one of her books.

Sir Mortimer Wheeler, the eminent archaeologist, tells of how she used to sit a little to one side at a party, looking upon the world with:

Calm and kindly eyes, observant rather than inquisitive, and always with a twinkle or a smile.

He describes her as essentially a shy presence, but her talk was 'easy and leisurely' with an occasional flash of wit.

A.L. Rowse, historian and writer, was a friend of Agatha's second husband and a frequent visitor to their home in Wallingford. He described her as having 'old-fashioned courtesy and good manners, very much a lady'. He too commented on her silences in which you were aware that she was taking everything in, and the fact that she could see right through people. He said that her intuition was alarming. He also wrote of her kindness, and was very complimentary about her first-class brain, and the fact that she had an extraordinary combination of perception and common sense. Physically, he noted that when young she had been a beautiful Teutonic blonde. In old age, she looked more like a large German Frau.

A next-door neighbour to Agatha Christie in the Lawn Road flats during the 1940s said that he used to pass her in the corridor, and described her as 'a cuddly looking, comfortable lady who one felt was much more likely to grow roses in her back garden than write detective novels'.

Francis Wyndham interviewed Agatha Christie for the London *Sunday Times* in February 1966. He described her as a large, quite tall woman wearing 'her grey hair pulled back into an enormous French knot at the back of her head, and her blue eyes sparkle from behind her glasses'. Her sense of humour was apparent during the conversation, and she admitted to him that she was slightly awed and bemused with the idea that she must produce a Christie for Christmas each and every year, describing herself with a quiet chuckle as a 'veritable sausage machine':

When you cut the string, another sausage begins to form.

One thing that is without question is Agatha Christie's incredible brainpower. When once questioned by her play director Peter Saunders about progress with regards to a certain play, she announced that it was all finished. When he asked when he would be able to see the script, she replied that it was only finished in her head, and she had yet to put it down onto paper.

When Wallace Douglas was asked to direct one of her plays, he went through the script and made four sides of notes on points he wanted to discuss. Having never met Agatha

Christie before, he was slightly nervous about mentioning over 100 points, but he knew that if he was to direct the play, he had to have confidence in it. He duly embarked on the list, carrying on relentlessly until he reached the end, nearly two hours later. Agatha took the feedback well, and they agreed on a deadline for the amended script. As he was leaving, Douglas asked Agatha whether she would like to take his list with her so that she could remember the changes suggested, but she said that wouldn't be necessary. On the date the script was promised, it arrived with every change made. Douglas got out his original list and was amazed to see that she had incorporated every single change from memory.

At Agatha Christie's memorial service, Sir William Collins of the Collins publishing empire who had been her publishers for most of her life, said 'the world was a better place because she lived in it'.

• AGATHA CHRISTIE AS SHE SAW HERSELF •

Agatha Christie was an extremely modest person. She said that she regarded her work as of no importance and she never saw herself as a literary figure. She said that she has simply been out to entertain and saw herself as someone with the faculty to amuse.

When discussing the success of her play, *The Mousetrap*, she admitted to being haunted by a feeling of being a fraud, with no right to call herself an author, and of simply playing an authorial role and 'making a mess of it into the bargain!' In her 40s, she said that it would never occur to her, when filling in a form, to put anything other than 'married woman' as her occupation.

Agatha said that people thought writing must be easy for her – it wasn't, it was murder. She claimed not to have written a book which she hadn't abandoned in disgust halfway through, and she said that she had never had much faith in her writing. She was always scared that one day people would find her out and discover that she really couldn't write at all.

However in the later life, shortly before her death in 1976, she did admit to Lord Snowdon that she would like it to be said that she was a 'good writer of detective and thriller stories'.

She sometimes showed a deep sense of inferiority and inadequacy. She told Lord Snowdon:

Well I am not an intellectual.

She often referred to herself as a 'lowbrow', compared to her intellectual husband Max who was a 'highbrow'. When she was awarded a CBE (Commander of the British Empire) in 1956, she exclaimed with glee that it was:

One up for the lowbrows!

When she wrote to A.L. Rowse regarding his discoveries about Shakespeare, she put:

From the mistress of low-brow detection to the master of
high-brow detection.

A story that is revealing in terms of her own self-perception
occured when, shortly after meeting Max Mallowan for the first
time, he accompanied her back home on the train journey from
Baghdad. Max sat opposite her in the carriage as she dozed, and
she awoke to find Max studying her thoughtfully. He told her that
he thought she had a really noble face. This astonished her as she
would never have thought of describing herself as such. She supposed that she did have a Roman nose, which would give her a
slightly noble profile, but she wasn't too sure she liked the idea
of a noble face. She mused that she was many things: 'good tem-
pered, exuberant, scatty, forgetful, shy, affectionate, completely
lacking in self-confidence, moderately unselfish but not noble'.
She relapsed into sleep, rearranging her Roman nose to look its
best, which in her view was full face rather than profile.

In later life, Agatha Christie looked back with nostalgia to
her early 20s when she was slim and active. She never ceased to
mourn this youthful self and had a horror of being photographed.
She would give her autograph generously, but never a photograph. She described herself in her autobiography as '13 stone of
solid flesh and what could only be described as a 'kind face''.

As a girl, Agatha worried because she was not talkative.
Although she enjoyed dancing, she did not enjoy having to
make conversation with her dance partner and found it very

uncomfortable. During a three-month trip to Egypt, one captain in the 60th Rifles returned Agatha to her mother after dancing with her and commented that, although she could dance, her mother now needed to teach her to talk.

She considered herself to be socially inept and was certainly not at ease at social functions. She had great admiration for those women who were. She yearned to be a clever, elegant conversationalist, 'flitting through parties in a silken ensemble'. In *Come, Tell Me How You Live*, she confessed that she looked with envy at self-possessed women who would flip cigarette ash around, while she crept miserably round the room at cocktail parties finding a place to hide her untasted glass. In an age when smoking was considered elegant, she tried for six months to learn to like smoking, religiously smoking a cigarette after lunch and dinner, but she never learnt to like it, and so gave up.

Her shyness meant that she hated any form of public speaking. When *The Mousetrap* became the longest-running play in the history of British theatre, she couldn't escape making a speech, but started:

I'm not good at speeches. I would rather write ten plays than make one speech.

Agatha Christie said that being inarticulate, writing was a great comfort and consolation to anyone like her, who was unsure of themselves and had trouble expressing themselves well in any other way.

Outside of her close circle of family and friends, she said that she preferred to speak with men rather than with women as she believed that 'men have much clearer brains and are not as cluttered up as women'.

The most revealing insight into her likes and dislikes came when she participated in a book published in 1973. *The Michael Parkinson's Confession Album* (published by Sidgwick & Jackson) contained the confessions, like and dislikes of many famous people. These are some of Agatha Christie's responses:

My ideal value: courage

My idea of beauty in nature: a bank of primroses in spring

My favourite study: astrology and aspects of history

My favourite flower: Lily of the Valley

My favourite colour: green

My favourite qualities in men: integrity and good manners

My favourite qualities in women: loving and merry

My greatest happiness: listening to music

My greatest misery: noise and long vehicles on roads

My favourite engagement: a good play

My favourite residence: my own home

My favourite authors: Elizabeth Bowen, Graham Greene

My favourite poets: T.S. Eliot, Yeats, Tennyson

My favourite classical composer: Elgar, Sibelius, Wagner

My favourite actors and plays: Alec Guinness, *Murder in the Cathedral*

My favourite animal: dogs

My favourite names: Isabella, Charles, Rodney

My favourite quotation: Life is a pure flame and we live by an
     invisible sun within us – Sir Thomas Browne

My favourite state of mind: peaceful

My motto: the business of life is to go forwards – Samuel
     Johnson

Aware of her own faults, mainly untidiness, soon after she
agreed to marry Max she laughingly promised to practise
being tidy tomorrow and punctual the day after.

In July 1971, Agatha Christie fell and broke her hip.
However, such was the character of the lady that she carried
on as usual for a week, believing that is was only badly bruised
and not wanting to make any fuss.

In the Epilogue of her autobiography, Agatha confirmed
that two lifetime ambitions had been fulfilled – the first was
dining with Queen Elizabeth II, and the second was being the
proud owner of a bottle-nosed Morris – 'a car of my own!'

• Agatha Christie's Favourites •

Agatha Christie enjoyed good food, travel, and spending
time with friends and family. She enjoyed swimming, playing
tennis until well into old age, and had loved golf until her first
husband, Archie, became an addict of the game.

She was an excellent card player, with numerous references to the game of Bridge in her books, and she loved cryptic crosswords and mathematical puzzles. When accompanying her second husband Max on archaeological digs in Iraq, her publishers used to fly copies of *The Times* out to her and, sitting outside a tent in Baghdad in 120°F heat, she could often be found doing *The Times'* crossword puzzle.

HER OWN BOOKS

Agatha Christie's second husband, Max Mallowan, wrote in his memoirs that fans often used to write to his wife asking which of her books was her favourite. Although her opinions changed from time to time, she would usually mention:

- *The Murder of Roger Ackroyd* (1926)
- *The Pale Horse* (1961)
- *The Moving Finger* (1943)
- *Crooked House* (1949)
- *Endless Night* (1967)

Max admitted that *Endless Night* was also his favourite because of the way in which Agatha obviously had such a clear psychological understanding of a twisted character who had a chance of choosing between good and evil, and chose the latter.

Agatha listed her favourite books as being *The Murder of Roger Ackroyd*, *The Pale Horse*, *The Moving Finger*, *Crooked House* and *Endless Night*.

One of Agatha's own special favourites was *Crooked House*. In the preface to the book, she said that she had been saving up the idea for years, working it through in her head, waiting until she had plenty of time as she really wanted to enjoy herself writing it. Indeed, when the *Daily Mail* asked on her 80th birthday what the favourite book that she had written was, she confirmed *Crooked House*.

In 1949, NBC Radio in New York dropped their plans to broadcast *Crooked House* as a Saturday evening serial, telling her agent it was because of the continuing complaints that they were getting from members of the public about the number of murders being committed on the air!

Of her foreign travel novels, she considered that *Death on the Nile* (1937) was one of her best. Her favourite collection of stories was *The Mysterious Mr Quin* (1930), and she considered the opening chapter of *The Body in the Library* (1942) to be the best she had ever written.

OTHER PEOPLE'S BOOKS

In a 1974 interview with Lord Snowdon, shortly before her death, she told how she loved to read Graham Greene's novels. She said that they were the sort of books that you couldn't put down because he wrote them so well.

As a teenager, she had been fascinated by Arthur Conan Doyle's detective stories involving Sherlock Holmes and said that she could read these for hours. Another key influence during her formative years was Charles Dickens' work. She commented that she enjoyed them because you could never really tell where the story was going. She felt that Dickens got bored of his characters halfway through a story and so just decided to add some more, 'but the new ones were just as wonderful'.

However, the number of characters in Dickens' novels caused her some problems of her own when she was asked by MGM to adapt her favourite Dickens' novel, *Bleak House*, into a film screenplay. She found that she had to cut out many of the best characters from the 800-page novel, but she tackled the task with great enthusiasm and was able to highlight the detective streak, which she said was always to be found somewhere in Dickens' stories. She completed her 270-page draft script in April 1962, but was told by MGM that it was too long for a two-hour film, which would normally be about 100 pages. Despite paying Agatha £10,000 for her services, the film was ultimately abandoned. Agatha commented that she had never got headaches before from worry over her work but, nonetheless, she had found the whole project fascinating.

She considered Elizabeth Bowen as one of the finest female writers ever, and thought that Muriel Spark and Ngaio Marsh wrote a very good detective story. Other contemporary detective writers that she favoured included Elizabeth Daly, Michael Gilbert and Patricia Highsmith. She was less enthusiastic about detective fiction that included violence and brutality.

Perhaps surprisingly, she thought that science fiction was quite enjoyable. She was not a fan, however, of Ian Fleming, finding his books incredibly boring!

FOOD

Agatha Christie adored good food, and saw it as one of life's greatest pleasures. She had no hesitation in describing herself as greedy, but lamented the impact that such good living had on her figure, describing herself as a 'fat old lady with piano legs'. Hubert Gregg, the director on a number of her plays, said that he had never seen a woman eat more, nor enjoy it more.

Amongst her favourite foods were boiled silverside and dumplings, seafood in a cream sauce, devilled lobster, garden-fresh vegetables, rice pudding made with cream, apple pie, elaborate chocolate cakes and Devonshire cream teas.

Apples were another favourite and she even had a special shelf built along the bath in Greenway (her home in Devon) so that she had somewhere to put the apples whilst she bathed.

She was an avid collector of recipes and an accomplished amateur cook. She was a whizz at making her own mayonnaise according to her butler George Gowler. However, she once told Marcelle Bernstein, a fellow member of the Detection Club, that she wouldn't want to do the cooking all the time – she would rather miss the servants!

Even when living in the desert on archaeological digs, she would dress for dinner and had Stilton cheese and chocolate truffles imported by her agent. Agatha thought that the best breakfast in the world was sausages cooked over a primus stove in the desert.

However, she never drank alcohol, and was a complete tee-totaller because she simply did not like the taste. Max, who loved fine wines, set out to educate her when they married, beginning with sweet Sauternes, then moving on to Clarets and Burgundies. They then tried vodka and absinthe, but she could not understand the fuss. Instead she would prefer a cup of cream to drink, or apple juice.

GARDENING

As a child, she would wander for hours in the gardens at Ashfield, her childhood home, and her passion for gardens continued all her life. A nearby neighbour to Ashfield was the West Country author, Eden Phillpotts, who used to show her around his garden of exotic plants and they used to weave stories together about the lands where these plants had come from.

She spent a great deal of time and money restoring the 33 acres of gardens at Greenway back to their former glory, and established extensive kitchen gardens and ornamental gardens. She loved to arrange the flowers from her garden around the house, filling her home with colourful blossoms and displays.

She took great pride in the Greenway gardens and from the 1950s started to enter lots of local flower and produce shows. Peter Saunders tells of the time when she won nearly all the prizes at the local Brixham Fruit and Vegetable Show, and when asked the secret of her success, she replied, 'my gardener'. In the end, after years of winning, Agatha Christie tactfully withdrew from entering.

Greenway House, Devon, stands on a plateau overlooking the River Dart.

In 1938, Agatha bought Greenway House, near Dartmouth, South Devon, with its 38 acres of gardens on the banks of the River Dart. She described it as her dream house.

TRAVEL

In 1922, as a young and newly married woman, Agatha Christie and her first husband Archie went on a ten-month round-the-world trip with their friend Major Belcher, who was charged with promoting the 1924 British Empire Exhibition. She visited South Africa, Australasia, Honolulu and Canada, and said later that the most beautiful country she had ever visited was New Zealand. She described the round-the-world trip as one of the most exciting things that had ever happened to her, and it started a lifelong love of travel.

ARCHAEOLOGY

Agatha Christie's interest in archaeology also started during her round-the-world trip. In South Africa, she was fascinated by the discovery of skulls and crude Bushman tools found in the Veldt. Shortly after her marriage to Archie ended, her first solo trip abroad was to Baghdad where she visited an archaeological site at Ur. It was on her second trip there, a year later, that she was to meet her second husband, Max Mallowan.

An archaeologist who went to visit the Mallowans at one of their archaeological digs in Iraq commented on how different Agatha was from when he had met her in England. In England she had been extremely shy; in Iraq she was a woman who was accepted at face value, not as a successful and famous authoress. She worked diligently, photographing and mending the archaeological finds in temperatures sometimes as high as 120°F. He also described her as being mainly responsible for the good humour that prevailed on the digs.

It is clear how much she loved those days on the dig with Max from her autobiographical travel book *Come, Tell Me How You Live*. The book provides an account of day-to-day life on an archaeological expedition to North Syria. She explained that when on a dig, she emerged from herself into her husband's work, but when at home, she retreated into herself to write her fiction. This book was published in 1946 under both of her married names – Agatha Christie Mallowan.

Agatha was not only an eager and willing participant in the archaeological digs, but was willing to put her hand in her pocket and finance them when they got into financial difficulties. In one particularly difficult year, Agatha donated the manuscript of *A Pocket Full of Rye* to ensure that the expedition survived financially.

As one might expect, the archaeological scene that played such a major role in her married life also featured in her detective stories. In the preface to *Death Comes as the End* (1945), Agatha tells how Professor Stephen Glanville, an archaeologist at the University of London, gave her the idea for a detective novel set in Thebes in 2000 BC. She researched and reconstructed an entire way of life in Ancient Egypt, including the mundane trivia and details. The credibility of the day-to-day life that she created provides the perfect background to the murder mystery.

THEATRE & MUSIC

Agatha Christie was an avid theatre goer. As a child, she had often attended the theatre and pantomime, and this gave her a valuable insight into the importance of dialogue, which was so vital to the success and readability of her books.

In later life, she loved to stay home in the evenings and listen to classical music. Although educated at home, music was the one area in which she had been taught professionally. She had a natural ability in playing the piano and was willing to practise for six hours a day, in an effort to achieve a professional standard. She played Mozart, Brahms and Beethoven exceptionally well, according to her husband Max. Whilst her ambition as a young teenager was to become a professional concert pianist, one of her music masters told her that she did not have the temperament to be a professional and carry the audience with her as she performed.

However, her shyness and self-consciousness when playing the piano to an audience disappeared when she sang. Gifted with a beautiful high soprano voice, she harboured dreams of becoming an opera singer, but once again her ambitions were thwarted as her teachers told her she did not possess the necessary volume of voice to become a professional.

Agatha shared her sister's love for the operas of Richard Wagner, and would make frequent trips to the opera, and in later life with her grandson Mathew.

DOGS

Agatha Christie was a lifelong lover of dogs. Her first dog Toby, a Yorkshire Terrier, was given to her as a present for her fifth birthday.

Another terrier, this time wire-haired, called Peter, became Agatha's constant and most loyal support during the traumatic days of her marriage breakdown and divorce. She described herself as going through a very hard time with nothing but a dog to cling to. *The Mystery of the Blue Train*, which was published in 1928 following her disappearance, was dedicated to:

Two Distinguished Members of the FOD, Carlotta and
Peter [her secretary and her dog].

People she knew were divided into the FOD (Faithful Order
of Dogs) and the FOR (Faithless Order of Rats) as she came
to find out who could really be relied on in tough times.

There were always dogs in Agatha's life. In later years, her
dogs seemed to be slightly more temperamental and neurotic.
Her husband Max described one dog, Treacle, as a snappy
little dog who was devoted to his mistress, and who made several abortive attempts on Max's ankles.

However, the most neurotic, troublesome and renowned
dog amongst visitors to Winterbrook (her home in
Oxfordshire) was Bingo, who adored Agatha and protected
her vigorously by biting some of her guests. A Manchester
terrier, black and tan, he was very noisy, and would snap and
bite. If he came sniffing around you, you were advised not to
move as he might bite. As a result, Max and Agatha would put
Bingo on a lead if anyone came to visit. One regular visitor to
Winterbrook asked Max why they put up with such a dog, and
Max replied that as well as bringing a lot of joy, he thought that
they would have found an easy conventional dog uninteresting.

Bingo did have his uses though – when a burglar climbed a
ladder into Agatha's bedroom, he only made off with a couple
of old fur coats as Bingo furiously interrupted his plans.

CARS AND DRIVING

Agatha's initial success as a writer meant that one of her first extravagant purchases was a motor car. She writes in her autobiography of the sheer joy of driving, of being able to visit places previously out of reach, and the freedom to go wherever she liked. She wrote that she did not think that anything gave her greater pleasure, or more joy of achievement than her bottle-nosed Morris Cowley.

In later life, she was not extravagant. The only Rolls-Royce they owned was purchased by Max, an old Phantom III Rolls-Royce, but it was sold shortly afterwards when he realised how impractical it was and how much petrol it used up!

COLLECTIBLES AND *OBJETS D'ART*

From her father, Agatha Christie inherited a lifetime passion for collecting objects, such as china, slagware, papier-mâché furniture, boxes and *objets d'art*. She describes her household as a family of collectors. When her mother visited Agatha in Paris, where she was at finishing school, they spent their visit looking for antique miniatures and silhouettes to add to their collection.

During her time as a pharmacist during the Second World War at University College Hospital, she began another one of her collecting hobbies. Since medicine bottles were in short supply, a charity used to organise a bottle rescue operation and deliver old bottles to the pharmacy. Agatha would always look out for any odd shaped bottles that could not be used for medicine, as she was allowed to take these home. They were then filled with eosin, copper sulphate, acriflavine, gentian violet, and other brightly coloured liquids to decorate the simple flat she was living in at the time at Lawn Road.

CRICKET

Another of her father's influences was to give Agatha a life-long love of cricket. As a child she used to accompany her father every Saturday morning during the season to the Torquay Cricket Club, where he was official scorer.

Half a century later, weekend guests to Greenway would be invited to participate in a family cricket match on a homemade pitch. Despite being a heavily built middle-aged woman, Agatha was never shy of having a go herself.

When her grandson Mathew was chosen to captain Eton's First XI at Lords Cricket Ground, Agatha was so proud that she declared it one of the great days of her life. After her death, the tour of the England Young Cricketers Club to the West Indies was mainly financed by Agatha Christie Ltd due to provisions made in her will.

ROYALTY

As a huge fan of royalty, Agatha Christie admitted that one of the highlights of her life was the evening she was invited to Buckingham Palace to dine with the Queen.

Queen Elizabeth II showed her appreciation for Agatha's work on New Year's Day in 1956 when she bestowed on her the Commander of the Order of the British Empire (CBE). Unable to attend because she was travelling in Africa on holiday, Agatha wrote that it was, once again:

One up to the lowbrows!

But it amused her that the Iraqi press had started to incorrectly refer to her as 'Dame'.

It was not until 1971 that the Queen granted her a DBE and she became Dame Agatha Christie. She described receiving her CBE and DBE as among the most satisfactory of her life. Only the knighthood conferred on her husband Max Mallowan in 1968 for services to archaeology gave her greater pleasure.

• AGATHA CHRISTIE AS AN EMPLOYER •

According to her biographer Gwen Robyns, although she was never known to pay high wages, there existed a great deal of friendship and respect between Agatha Christie and her employees.

Agatha grew up in an upper-middle-class family, in a spacious house with a large staff of servants. It was still considered normal to have 'staff' when Agatha married Archie Christie. It was not just a case of the rich people having servants – they just had more of them!

During their early married life, Agatha and Archie were most definitely not rich. However, even though Archie was only earning a modest City salary, Agatha employed a maid-of-all-work and also a nurse for her daughter, Rosalind. She commented in later life that it seemed odd that a young couple who were unable to afford a motor car, to buy new clothes, take a taxi on a rare evening out, or entertain their more affluent friends, should still find it essential to hire two full-time servants. Spending priorities in those days appear to have been dictated by class prejudice, rather than financial logic, according to Gillian Gill.

Agatha employed a variety of staff over the years. At Ashfield, her childhood home which she kept after her mother's death, Agatha also kept on the services of Florence Potter who was to remain her cook and housekeeper for fifteen years. In an interview with Florence Potter's son Freddie in the Torquay's *Herald Express* in 1990, he recalls how his mother used to provide four meals a day, on a daily basis during the summer months when Agatha was in residence; and when she was entertaining, it would usually be a seven-course meal.

In researching her book, talking to people who had known Agatha, Gwen Robyns was told that the whole atmosphere of

Ashfield was congenial, and Agatha had the ability to put children, staff and tradesmen at ease – all workmen were treated with the utmost courtesy.

One member of staff who remained loyally with Agatha during the 1950s at her house in Devon, Greenway, was George Gowler. George was actually a chef, but he had seen an advert for 'a butler and his wife, working for a writer'. After an interview with Mrs Christie in her London flat in Swan Court, he was hired for the position. Undaunted by his lack of experience as a butler, he found a little booklet entitled 'How to be a Butler' at a bookstall at Paddington station, on his way down to Greenway for the first time, and that was the start of his career!

Later in life, Gowler gave talks about Agatha's life and works, whilst dressed in his original butler's outfit. He was able to give many insights into life working for Agatha Christie. The highlight of the day had been the evening meal, which could sometimes last for over two and a half hours. The evening started with drinks in the library, and twenty minutes before dinner was due, Gowler would strike a gong to give people time to change for dinner.

The tradition was that if Gowler was in the mood, and everything had gone well that day, he would dress in his full butler's uniform to strike the gong. Someone would come out of the library to see what Gowler was wearing. If it was his full uniform, then everyone would dress up for dinner. However, if the day had been 'a bit messy', he would wear black trousers and white coat, which meant that the dress code for dinner was casual.

• Agatha Christie as a Playwright and Author •

Behind her twinkling eyes and charmingly shy manners, Agatha Christie could be awkward, obstinate and a perfectionist when it came to her work.

Right from the start of her career, her letters to her editors were crisp and business-like. As Gwen Robyns points out, they were 'not the letters of a shy young author, but a woman completely in charge of herself and her career'.

Her editors claimed that she would strongly protest at the altering of any words in her manuscripts, because it was important to her what the characters sounded like and said. Dialogue was key to her detective stories, and she would not tolerate it being altered. When it was pointed out to her that she had made a mistake about the motor route from Charing Cross to Ascot, she willingly agreed that:

Miss Howse was quite right and you wouldn't go through Ealing and Hanwell.

However, she was not so accommodating when Insurance Company was altered to Assurance Company, which she thought 'quite unnecessary'.

Agatha also knew what she wanted for the covers of her books and insisted on getting it. When she did not like the proposed cover for her third book, *Murder on the Links* (1923), she visited the offices of her publishers in person to explain that the proposed cover had absolutely no connection with the plot of her book. The cover was duly altered.

Neither was she happy with the cover for her next book, *The Man in the Brown Suit*. She wrote to the publisher that the cover looked nothing like a tube station, and 'more like a highway robbery and murder in medieval times'. She insisted that the cover be given 'a background of white glossy tiles, which everyone could identify as being a typical London Underground station', the book's initial setting.

Agatha also showed a keen understanding of public relations, as she pressurised her publishers to get *Poirot Investigates* published whilst there was still fresh publicity around from the 1923 *Sketch* article and the serialisation of *The Man in the Brown Suit* by the *London Evening News*.

When it came to her work as a playwright, Agatha Christie was no less meticulous. She had an excellent relationship with Peter Saunders, who produced her plays for the stage. They respected each other's judgement, understood each other, and had a genuine friendship, which meant that Peter Saunders could give her advice that she would never have accepted from anyone else.

Hubert Gregg, who directed several of Agatha's plays, recalled an incident at the rehearsal for *The Hollow*. One of the actors was consistently mispronouncing a word. Gregg and the actor got into a debate as to whether the word should be per*emp*tory (the actor's pronunciation) or *per*emptory (Gregg's version). Agatha Christie spoke up in the actor's defence, and bet Hubert Gregg a pound that the actor was saying the word correctly. The next day Agatha turned up and quietly took her usual seat. With a wink, she handed Hubert Gregg a one pound note. She wasn't above admitting a mistake!

According to Gwen Robyns, it was one of Agatha Christie's endearing qualities that she was loyal to her professional friends and rarely made any changes. Peter Saunders was to produce her plays for over thirty years, Edmund Cork was to remain her agent for over fifty years, and after an initial mistake in selecting her first publisher, she switched to Collins who were to remain her publisher for a similar period. She also retained the same solicitors, Hooper and Wollen of Torquay, who attended to all her mother's affairs.

• AGATHA CHRISTIE AS A MEMBER OF THE COMMUNITY •

Whilst living at Greenway, Agatha Christie involved herself in both the village and the parish. However, she was more elusive when living at Wallingford, and during her thirty years there few people ever saw her. She was however president of the local amateur dramatic group for twenty-six years, and so the best way to catch a glimpse of Lady Mallowan, as she was known locally following her second husband Max's knighthood, was to book seats for the Christmas pantomime which she always tried to attend.

Agatha's sympathy was always practical. When she heard of one old lady in her village who was struggling financially, she ordered a box of groceries from the village shop to be delivered every week, for as long as the old lady was living.

At Greenway, Agatha was a regular attender at St Mary the Virgin church in nearby Churston Ferrers. She was a deeply religious woman, and gained strength and comfort from prayer during her lifetime. By her bedside she kept a copy of *The Imitation of Christ* by Thomas Kempis, just as her mother had done in her lifetime.

In 1955, she decided that she wanted to endow the church with a new stained-glass window, to replace the plain east window. In her autobiography, Agatha Christie wrote that possibly the one thing she had done that had given her the most pleasure was writing a story and donating the proceeds for a new stained-glass window in her local church. She described it as a beautiful little church and its plain-glass east window used to gape at her like a gap in the teeth. She wanted it to be a happy window which children could look at with pleasure. She said she was both proud and humbled that she was permitted to leave this legacy with the proceeds of her work.

Agatha asked that there be no indication that she was the donor, and she donated the royalties from her first short story in years 'Greenshaw's Folly' to the Exeter Diocesan Board of Finance for this purpose. She commissioned a stained-glass window showing Jesus as the Good Shepherd in her favourite colours of greens and mauves. The window was designed by a local craftsman and artist from Bideford,

St Mary the Virgin church in Churston Ferrers, Devon, where Agatha
Christie dedicated a new stained-glass window to the church.

James Patterson, who had assembled the window and was
keen to install it. However, there was a slight problem – no
one wanted to buy the Agatha Christie short story that was
supposed to pay for it.

According to Richard Hack, letters were sent between
Agatha's British and American agents:

I hate to be a pest, but the Bishop of Exeter's lawyers are
being horrid about Greenshaw's Folly. They say they find
it difficult to believe that Mrs Mallowan would have presented the church with a story that would not sell!

After months of trying, unsuccessfully, to sell the story to an American magazine, Agatha's agent in the UK, Edmund Cork, arranged to buy back the rights from the Church for £1,000 in early 1957. 'Obviously the window must go up,' he wrote to Agatha, when explaining his decision. Agatha found the whole incident very humiliating but correct. 'Greenshaw's Folly' was eventually included in the short-story collection, *The Adventure of the Christmas Pudding* (1960).

St Mary the Virgin church in Churston Ferrers was attended by Agatha's daughter Rosalind until her own death in 2004. Even though Agatha had asked that there be no indication that she was the donor, a plaque was unveiled by Rosalind after Agatha's death, saying that A.C. Mallowan DBE gave the east window 'to the glory of God'.

Agatha was also active in her role as governor of Galmpton Primary School, in the nearest village to Greenway. As the owner of Greenway, she was automatically appointed to the board of governors of the Church of England primary school. One of the first things she did was to give the school a 20ft-high silver birch tree for Christmas in 1940. She had the tree decorated with coloured lights and also bought a present for every schoolchild.

Agatha Christie introduced an annual essay writing competition for the school, to encourage the children in the art of writing. The Mallowan Literary Prize was awarded each year. She would set the subject matter, which ranged from, 'My Idea of a Hero', 'If You Were not Yourself who would you Like to Be', or 'My Favourite Character from the Bible'.

She insisted that the children enter using false names, so that she would not be influenced by those that she knew. She also told Mr Fellingham, the headmaster, that she tried not to be influenced by better handwriting and spelling. As a test, she used to put them in 'cold storage' and after a couple of weeks saw which one had stuck in her memory. It used to take Agatha three weeks each year to read through all the essays, and after she had whittled them down to a shortlist, Sir Allen Lane of Penguin Books joined her for the weekend to select the winner. The results were sent to the school with an accompanying letter which explained the reason for her choice of first prize.

On her 85th birthday, Agatha wrote to the then headmaster saying that she was handing over the position on the Board of Governors to her daughter, Rosalind. In 2009, the National Trust reintroduced the competition.

• AGATHA CHRISTIE AS A FAMILY MEMBER •

Most of the information on Agatha as a family member has come in recent years from her grandson, Mathew Prichard. Whilst she was alive, members of the family closely guarded Agatha's privacy. Agatha prized her family more than anything else.

Mathew called his grandmother 'Nima', probably based upon his first attempt at 'Grandma'. However, Nima seemed a completely appropriate nickname for Agatha, and therefore it became the universal family name for her. His first memory was of rushing downstairs far too early in the morning at Greenway to find Nima, in the hope that she would tell him stories about his two cuddly elephants, Butterfly and Flutterby.

In later life, he described his grandmother as modest with a great sense of humour. He saw her as:

Intensely shy, a very private kind of person, who listened more than she talked, who saw more than she was seen.

Her grandson's fondest memories are of the times when she had just finished writing her latest novel. As she did with many of her books, every night the family would gather in the drawing room of Greenway after dinner, and Agatha would sit in a deep chair with her butterfly shaped spectacles on and read a chapter or two of the book. Once she had finished her reading, each family member was invited in turn to guess the identity of the murderer. Agatha was keen to try out the book on a live audience to test its plot and plausibility. However every evening, Max would fall asleep during the reading, and would only wake up when prompted to guess the murderer. He always used to plump for the most unlikely suspect and then go back to sleep again. This used to infuriate Agatha, because quite often his guesses were correct!

Mathew also tells of his school friends' reaction to meeting his famous grandmother. Whilst he did not know what his friends were expecting, they were all impressed by her friendliness and modesty, but most of all by the interest she always took in what they themselves were doing.

Agatha Christie used to send her grandson a signed copy of her new book when it was released, to his boarding school. As usual, all books received were vetted by the headmaster before being given to the children. However, Mathew noticed that his books always took longer to be vetted than the books sent to other children by their parents and grandparents. He started to fret that maybe his grandmother had 'overstepped the limit with the level of violence that was acceptable to the headmaster'. However, he needn't have worried. It transpired that the headmaster's wife was a huge Agatha Christie fan, and always insisted on reading the book first, before it was given to Mathew.

• NICKNAMES & PSEUDONYMS •

Agatha grew up in a family which was always giving nick-names to family members and friends.

- Agatha herself was called Agatha-Pagatha by her father; and Nima by her grandson Mathew.
- Agatha's sister, Margaret, was known as Madge, and then in later life as Punkie.
- Agatha's daughter, Rosalind, was nicknamed Teddy.

They also gave nicknames to things as well – her old battered rocking horse was called Mathilde, and the potting shed was known as 'the K K'.

Whilst still a teenager, Agatha wrote her first novel, entitled *Snow Upon the Desert*. It was submitted to several publishers under the pseudonym 'Monosyllaba' but was never published.

Once she started to write detective novels, Agatha admitted that she was tempted to hide behind a male pseudonym in order to be taken seriously at first, as she felt that a woman's name would prejudice people against her work.

Since 1910 both Agatha and her sister had written occasional short stories for magazines. Madge Miller used the pseudonym 'Mack Miller', and Agatha Miller (as she was then) started sending stories to magazines under the pseudonym 'Daniel Miller'. Agatha also occasionally sent stories using her grandfather's name, Nathaniel Miller.

Indeed, these were the pseudonyms that she used when negotiating her Mary Westmacott publishing contract (see p.89), in order to keep her real identity private. Her daughter Rosalind revealed that this pseudonym was chosen after some thought. Mary was Agatha's second name, and Westmacott the name of some distant relatives. She managed to keep the Westmacott identity secret for over eighteen years.

• AGATHA CHRISTIE'S DESIRE FOR PRIVACY •

On Friday 3 December 1926, a shy, fun-loving woman who was grieving the death of her mother and was going through some major marital problems, disappeared for eleven days. The nation was gripped and fascinated by her disappearance and a nationwide manhunt was undertaken until she was eventually found staying at a hotel in Harrogate.

Although it was this notoriety that helped make Agatha Christie famous, she never recovered from the episode or the press interest in it, and turned overnight into a recluse, closely guarding her privacy. She carried her craving for privacy to greater lengths than any other writer of her generation.

Despite being offered lucrative rewards for television appearances and lecture tours, they were all firmly declined.

She sought to avoid any publicity whatsoever, and would not allow her publishers to give publicity parties or print a current photograph of her in her books. The small photograph that was permitted on the back of her books became thirty years out of date, and she refused to have a new photograph taken, to prevent any of her readers from recognising her in the street.

She granted fewer than ten interviews in her lifetime, and then only to select people who were certain not to ask about her private life or her disappearance. No matter how the questions differed, she always brought out her stock answers.

Her long-awaited autobiography was not published until after her death for this reason, and no mention is made of the episode which turned her from a moderately well-known author, to a household name. Her second husband, Max Mallowan, published his memoirs after her death but included very little more than had been stated in her own autobiography.

During Agatha's lifetime she had foiled any attempt by other authors to write her biography, even though she had seen that where no information existed about her, people made it up. She was regularly outraged by what she read about herself.

Unauthorised biographers, such as Gwen Robyns whose biography was published in 1978, were discouraged in their efforts by an uncooperative wall of silence from those who had been closest to Agatha Christie, and the inaccessibility of relevant documents. Robyns was even unable to listen to recordings held by the Imperial War Museum of Agatha's memories of the war because, even though the recording was part of a public institution's collection, she required authority from Agatha Christie's estate, which was not granted.

The Christie family finally broke its silence in the early 1980s, when Agatha's daughter Rosalind commissioned Janet Morgan to write an official biography of her mother's life.

However, many commentators, including Gillian Gill, felt that her lack of creation of a strong positive public image during her lifetime had a negative influence on the critical appreciation of her work, and as a result she has a poor literary reputation amongst critics.

~~~

Her shyness and desire for privacy meant that when she took an appointment within the dispensary at University College Hospital as part of the war effort in the summer of 1941, few people knew that there was such a famous person dispensing medicine in the out-patients department. In a memoir in the *Pharmaceutical Journal* after her death, Dr Harold Davis CBE recalled that she loved to exchange pleasantries with the patients, but he was often amused to conjecture at what those patients would have thought had they known their medicine had been compounded and presented to them by none other than Agatha Christie!

• AGATHA GIVING HERSELF AWAY IN HER BOOKS •

At the height of her fame with her detective novels and thrillers, unbeknownst to anyone including her closest friends, in 1928 Agatha started to write a series of novels under the pseudonym Mary Westmacott. These six novels seem to have been a form of therapy for Agatha Christie as she worked through some of the important issues in her life.

Her second husband Max, in his memoirs, said that, for all her impenetrable armour and defensive resistance to inquisitive probing, Agatha actually reveals herself in her Westmacott books. It is her second novel, *Unfinished Portrait* (1934), that was, according to her husband Max, an autobiography mixed with imagination. In it she examined her own marital breakdown with her first husband Archie. Max wrote that in this book:

> We have more clearly than anywhere else a portrait of Agatha.

Unfinished Portrait is the story of Celia, a thinly disguised version of the author. Episode after episode of the story is echoed in her autobiography – Celia's first few years of marriage to Dermot are happy, she begins to write books, and they have a daughter. However, the game of golf caused a separation of interest, and ends the early happy companionship of weekends. This played a key role in the breakdown of their marriage, with her husband's interests developing elsewhere.

In reality, her second husband Max said that until he read this book he was unable to understand the vehemence with which Agatha had made him promise not to play the game of golf!

In the book, Dermot tells Celia he wants a divorce because he's fallen in love with another woman and that the name of the other woman must not be mentioned. Celia suffers a mental breakdown, unable to contemplate life without him.

By examining both Agatha Christie's autobiography, published posthumously, and her novel *Unfinished Portrait*, we can gain clear insight into those autobiographical strains of the works and its candid reflections. It is possible to gain a greater understanding of the hidden Christie and the public Christie, for she emerges as a vulnerable individual, shaped by the forces of the family and the values of Edwardian society.

After maintaining her secret for eighteen years, Agatha Christie's cover as Mary Westmacott was blown in 1946 when an American review of her book *Absent in the Spring* (1944) revealed that it had actually been written by Agatha. Christie was wounded and outraged at her identity being revealed and told her agent that it 'was cramping to one's subject matter', and that an author's wishes really should have been respected.

A second way in which Agatha Christie reveals herself in her work, is through the lightly sketched and comic portrayal of herself in the detective Ariadne Oliver.

Mrs Oliver is first introduced in *The Case of the Discontented Soldier* (1934), working surrounded by untidy sheets of manuscript and with a passion for apples – characteristics that she shared with her creator. Ariadne Oliver is described by Gillian Gill as 'a large, untidy, scatter-brained, middle-aged woman' with a 'love of small, low-slung, fast cars completely at variance with her sex, age and ample figure'.

Ariadne is the creator of a Finnish detective called Sven Hjerson, and the authoress of forty-six successful works of fiction, all best-sellers, translated into many varied languages.

She sincerely regrets making him foreign as she is always getting letters from Finland pointing out something impossible that he has said or done. As time goes on, she grows to hate her detective more and more, tired of his mannerisms. In reality, Agatha admitted that she regretted creating Hercule Poirot as Belgian and would have happily killed Poirot off if it hadn't been for his great following of fans.

Ariadne Oliver hates making speeches (as does her creator), stating that she gets all worried and nervous, concerned that she will say the same thing twice. In later life she starts to physically resemble Agatha Christie, with 'wind-swept grey hair, an eagle profile' and ample figure.

Agatha Christie uses her alter-ego to protest about film-makers and dramatists who wish to change her detective's character, making him younger with an inappropriate love interest. Mrs Oliver also complains about the unfair tax system, which means the more she writes, the more it costs her. Indeed, in later times, Agatha Christie limited herself to just one book a year for this very reason.

Gillian Gill perfectly sums us the creation of Ariadne Oliver as 'a self-parody that is both comical and confident', but the character is written 'in such a way that we find ourselves laughing *with* her, rather than at her'.

• AGATHA CHRISTIE AS PROPERTY
OWNER & DEVELOPER •

At one point, Agatha Christie owned eight houses. She had a lifelong preoccupation with property, starting from childhood when her passion was doll's houses. House moves would be undertaken once a week, with a cardboard box on a piece of string as the furniture van. At one point, her dolls' house furniture collection grew so much that a large cupboard had to be converted into an enormous dolls' house.

Agatha Christie once admitted that, looking back on life, she could see that her tastes had stayed fundamentally the same and what she liked playing with as a child, she liked playing with as an adult – houses, for example! Her adult life revolved around the acquisition and restoration of houses, which was somewhat surprising for a woman of her era. Indeed, her autobiography opens with the words from a 1958 song by Jules Bruyères, 'My dear home, my nest, my house', and this choice of opening indicates the sense of security that she placed on her home.

Agatha Christie was born at Ashfield, 15 Barton Road, Torquay. She lived here throughout her childhood, and even after her marriage to Archibald Christie in 1914, she continued to live in Ashfield until after the First World War. Today all that remains to mark the spot where Ashfield once stood is a blue plaque set in stone, by the bus bay on Barton Road.

Above and left: Agatha was born at Ashfield, Barton Road, Torquay in 1890. Today all that remains to mark the spot is a blue plaque.

After the war had ended, housing was in short supply throughout London, so Agatha and Archie rented a series of flats in London:

---

* firstly a pair of rooms on the second floor of a large, decaying house at 5 Northwick Terrace, St John's Wood, just off Maida Vale, now demolished;
* then a short lease on a first floor, four-bedroomed furnished flat with two sitting rooms at 25 Addison Mansions, an apartment block behind Olympia in London, not far from Holland Park, costing 5 guineas per week. This building was later demolished to make way for Cadby Hall, Lyons' headquarters;
* followed by a move to a similar sized but more permanent unfurnished flat, again within Addison Mansions at No 96, on the fourth floor. Agatha had already signed a lease on a flat near Battersea Park when she discovered this second more suitable flat in Addison Mansions. So she suggested to her husband that they should rent out the Battersea flat for a premium. She refers to this moment as 'high financial genius' in her autobiography.

A move to the country was called for when Archie became obsessed with playing golf. First they rented one of four flats in a large converted Victorian House called Scotswood, in Sunningdale, Berkshire, 30 miles south-west of London so that Archie could still commute to his job in London.

With Agatha's writing career taking off, after two years living at Scotswood, they were able to buy a property for the first time in 1924 – a large house in the same town of Sunningdale. Agatha described the house as: 'A sort of millionaire-style Savoy suite' but in the country.

They renamed the house Styles, after Agatha's first book, *The Mysterious Affair at Styles*.

When they bought Styles, it was already lavishly decorated, with panelled walls and every other imaginable luxury. However, the house had a reputation of being an unlucky house, and had changed hands several times in previous years. The house's reputation was to prove correct, as Agatha and Archie were to divorce four years later.

After their marriage ended, Agatha put Styles and all its contents on the market for £5,500. Archie continued to live at Styles while it was on the market, but neither of them wanted to live there permanently any more.

Agatha then moved into a flat in Kensington High Street, London, with her daughter Rosalind and her secretary and close friend Carlotta. However, she continued to use her childhood home, Ashfield, as a base after her divorce and then as her summer home right through until 1938.

In 1929, Agatha Christie purchased a pretty mews house at 22 Cresswell Place, Chelsea, London, just south of the Old Brompton Road. With the help of a builder, Agatha made some substantial alterations, knocking down walls and rearranging the downstairs to incorporate an area which had previously been a horse stable. She turned it into a comfortable, charming but cramped home, and decorated it herself from top to bottom. Agatha was to own this property for the rest of her life, although she often rented out her properties when she was no longer using them herself. It is still there, with a blue plaque commemorating her ownership.

Above and right: In 1929 Agatha Christie purchased 22 Cresswell Place, Chelsea, London. She was to own this property for the rest of her life.

DAME
AGATHA
CHRISTIE
1890-1976
Author
lived here

After she and Max returned from honeymoon in 1934, they set about furnishing their new purchase, a house at 58 Sheffield Terrace, Campden Hill in London W8, just off Kensington Church Street. In her autobiography, she incorrectly states that it was 48 Sheffield Terrace that she owned, but when English Heritage went to award the property a Blue Plaque in 2001, they discovered her name on the electoral register for 58 Sheffield Terrace.

The house at Sheffield Terrace was originally two houses, which had been turned into one property. Spread over three floors, it had a carved lion and unicorn over the front door, and a roof garden. On the third floor was Agatha's private study and music room, with a Steinway grand piano, a table and chair, to allow Agatha to type, and one sofa and armchair – nothing else, not even a telephone. This was to become Agatha's sanctuary – a room of her own.

Agatha loved the spaciousness of the property. The property was also close to Notting Hill Gate underground station and so was convenient for Max's commute to the British Museum, where he was working. However, the property suffered during the bombings of the Second World War, and her Steinway was 'never quite the same afterwards!'.

Max shared her delight in domesticity and her interest in buying houses. During the 1930s, Agatha went on a property-buying spree, and shortly before the start of the Second World War, she was the proud owner of eight houses. In her autobiography she admitted to being addicted to finding run down

Agatha purchased 58 Sheffield Terrace, Campden Hill in London in 1934. Spread over three floors, it had a carved lion and unicorn over the front door and a roof garden with a private study for Agatha on the third floor.

'slummy' houses in London, particularly the Kensington and Chelsea areas, and doing them up. She would then live in them for a year or two, renting out the previous one, before moving on to the next. They apparently showed a good profit when she sold them, and she described it as:

An enjoyable holiday while it lasted.

As well as purchasing Sheffield Terrace in 1934, in the December, Agatha and Max bought a five-bedroomed Queen Anne house about a mile west outside of Wallingford. They bought it just before departing on a trip to Syria for an archae-ological dig, and so did not see it again for nine months. Called Winterbrook House, it had a river frontage onto the Thames, but was also right on the road. A.L. Rowse, who was a friend of Max's and a frequent visitor to Winterbrook, explained that they were not disturbed by any traffic noise due to heavy shrubbery in the front, and the fact that the rooms they occu-pied were mainly at the back of the house, leading onto the garden and the meadows which swept down to the river. Rowse described it as a sunny house, always warm and cosy.

Agatha and Max used Winterbrook as a country cot-tage for the weekends as it was easier to reach than Devon. Agatha however always regarded this as Max's house as it was easily accessible to his beloved Oxford, where he had been to university, and was later in life to become a Fellow of All Souls' College.

Above and right: Agatha's five-bedroomed Winterbrook House, about a mile west outside of Wallingford, Oxfordshire.

OXFORDSHIRE BLUE PLAQUES BOARD

Dame
AGATHA CHRISTIE
1890-1976

Author
lived here 1934-76
with her husband
SIR MAX MALLOWAN
1904-1978
Archaeologist

In summer 1938, Agatha Christie sold her childhood home of Ashfield as the suburbs of Torquay had started to encroach upon her beloved house. Instead, she bought Greenway House in Churston Ferrers, South Devon, not far from Dartmouth. When Agatha asked the price of the property, she assumed that she had misheard, expecting them to be asking £16,000 for it, rather than the astonishing £6,000 that was the actual price.

Agatha and Max bought the property on 28 October 1938, with its 33 acres and land down to the River Dart. Her architect suggested that the property's newer Victorian additions be removed, and although this would reduce the property size by about one third, it would restore it to its original delightful Georgian design. Max, in his memoirs, said that Agatha, with her genius for decorating houses, 'made it a thing of beauty'.

The boathouse overlooking the River Dart, Greenway, Devon.

In her own autobiography, Agatha tells how, when she was growing up, she and her mother had always thought Greenway to be 'the most perfect of all the houses on the Dart'. It was to become her summer residence from 1938 until her death, and she featured it in several of her books – most notably *Dead Man's Folly* (1956) and *Five Little Pigs* (1943). The property's boathouse is on the spot where it is said Sir Walter Raleigh, while smoking tobacco, had a jug of ale thrown over him by a servant who thought he was on fire.

Agatha Christie described Greenway variously as 'idyllic', 'her ideal house' and her 'dream house' in her beloved Devon. However, biographer Gwen Robyns believes it is doubtful that Agatha would ever have liked to have lived in Devon on a permanent basis. She was a restless woman who enjoyed a regular change of scenery, spending part of her year in Devon, part in London, part in Wallingford, and part abroad with Max on his archaeological digs.

Not long after they purchased Greenway, however, the Second World War broke out. On 31 August 1942, Agatha wrote to Max to tell him that the Admiralty were taking over the property. In 1943, Greenway was requisitioned for use as officers' quarters for the United States navy. It wasn't until Christmas Day 1946 that they finally took back possession of the house from the Admiralty.

The occupation by the American naval officers left no last-ing damage, apart from the addition of fourteen lavatories which were installed beside the kitchen! One of the officers, Lt Marshall Lee, had painted a frieze around the library, show-ing all the places his unit had travelled, ending with a view of Greenway and the Dart. Agatha loved it, and it is retained to this day.

Agatha, who was working in London during the war, was forced to rent a series of properties, since her own extensive portfolio of properties were all let to either friends or ten-ants. She rented flats in Half Moon Street, Park Place just off St James Street, and 22 Lawn Road in Hampstead.

Agatha bought another property just after the war at Swan Court, just south of the Kings Road in Chelsea. It was Flat 48, in a large apartment block with an imposing arched entrance and central courtyard, and with the actress Dame Cybil Thorndike as a neighbour. Agatha would alternate between using Swan Court and Cresswell Place as her London home for the rest of her life.

Perhaps the most extreme indication of Agatha Christie's house mania and the sense of security she placed on having a home, is told in her book *Come, Tell Me How You Live*. This auto-biographical memoir was written about her archaeological experiences whilst accompanying her second husband, Max Mallowan, on his digs in Syria and Iraq in the 1930s. She writes in great detail about the house she and Max built – and as Professors Maida & Spornick surmise in their book – it is:

A home for a person who needed the security of a house, even in the desert.

Greenway House in Devon had been given to Agatha's daughter, Rosalind, in 1959, and she moved in with her second husband, Anthony Hicks in 1968. In 2000 Rosalind and Anthony agreed to give Greenway to the National Trust as a means of preserving and protecting the grounds and building. The gardens opened to the public in 2002, and in 2005, once both Rosalind and Anthony had died, the National Trust embarked on a £5.4 million restoration. In February 2009 it opened to the public.

Tour bus for Greenway House.

• ACKNOWLEDGMENT & RECOGNITION
FOR AGATHA CHRISTIE •

In 1950 Agatha Christie was appointed a Fellow of the Royal Society of Literature.

In 1955 she was awarded the Edgar Award (a small bust of Edgar Allan Poe) for Best Play from the Mystery Writers of America for *The Witness for the Prosecution*. Also that year she was the first recipient of the Mystery Writers of America's highest honour, The Grand Master Award, which recognised lifetime achievement and consistent quality.

On 1 January 1956, Agatha Christie was made a Commander of the British Empire (CBE) in the queen's New Year's Honours List.

In 1961, Agatha received an honorary degree from the University of Exeter. She was given an Honorary Doctorate of Letters, and was, therefore, entitled to use the initials DLitt after her name.

In 1971, at the age of 81, she was made Dame Commander of the British Empire, the female equivalent to a knighthood.

In 1972 a life-size wax figure of her was placed in Madame Tussaud's Wax Museum, sitting in the conservatory wearing clothes and shoes that Agatha had actually worn, seated below film director Alfred Hitchcock.

To mark the 100th anniversary of her birth in 1990, a bronze bust sculpted by Dutch artist Carol van den Boom-Cairns was unveiled by her daughter Rosalind in Cary Gardens, Torquay.

A bronze bust sculpted by Dutch artist Carol van den Boom-Cairns was unveiled in Cary Gardens, Torquay to mark the 100th anniversary of Agatha Christie's birth in 1990.

Agatha Christie Week was inaugurated in 2005 and takes place each September around her birthday. Torquay, where she was born, staged its first festival as part of it. The Agatha Christie Festival is now an annual event where fans from all over the world congregate to celebrate her life and work.

In terms of recognition from other authors and influential people:

The novelist Daphne du Maurier wrote to Agatha from her home in Cannes, telling Agatha that her paperbacks were in all the bookshops in Cannes, in both French and in English. However, much to Ms du Maurier's mortification, none of hers were; she was most put out!

Margery Allingham once said that Agatha Christie's success was 'because she appeals directly to the human curiosity in all of us'. She invites her readers to 'listen to the details surrounding the perfectly horrid screams from the apartment next door'. She also said that Agatha had 'entertained more people for more hours than almost any other writer of her generation'.

According to Hilary Macaskill, Agatha Christie was denounced by the Chinese communist press as a:

Running dog for the rich and powerful: she described crimes committed by the lower classes of British society, but never explained their social causes.

• PROTECTION OF AGATHA CHRISTIE'S INTEGRITY •

Agatha's daughter, Rosalind, and her grandson, Mathew, as chairman of Agatha Christie Ltd, worked hard to both protect and promote her work. In 1993, Rosalind founded the Agatha Christie Society to preserve the legacy of her mother's writings. Rosalind took the role of president, with Joan Hickson and David Suchet as vice presidents. She felt that David Suchet as Poirot and Joan Hickson as Miss Marple had come closer to the looks and spirit of their characters than any other actors. Her lifetime's aim was to ensure that her mother's works didn't suffer from excessive commercialisation or trivialisation.

Christie remains a strong presence in the publishing world, partly due to the purchase of Agatha Christie Ltd in 1998 by Chorion. Chorion, with its expertise in branding and global franchising, owned the rights of a multitude of characters from the Mr Men to the Famous Five. Chorion have now sold their 64 per cent stake in Agatha Christie Ltd to American home entertainment company Acorn Media. The remaining 36 per cent of Agatha Christie Ltd is retained by the Christie family.

In 1978 Kathleen Tynan wrote a novel, which was an imaginative solution to the mystery of Agatha's disappearance:

Agatha: A Mystery Novel. Before the book was even published, David Puttnam announced that he was adapting it into a film. This brought an indignant response from Agatha's daughter who wrote a letter to *The Times* complaining that the family had not been consulted about the forthcoming 'fairy-tale'. She said she found it 'particularly objectionable and morally beneath contempt'. Her legal challenge to prevent the filming of *Agatha* (1979) was unsuccessful, and Vanessa Redgrave played Christie.

3

POIROT VS MARPLE

· HERCULE POIROT ·

Appearing in thirty-three novels and fifty-three short stories, including Agatha's first published novel *The Mysterious Affair at Styles* (1920), Hercule Poirot is a Belgian detective who has retired from his career in the police force, and is in his 60s when we first meet him.

Born in Belgium in the 1840s, he was an only child. In *Three Act Tragedy* (1935) Poirot for the first and only time discusses his youth with Mr Satterthwaite. He had been a poor boy and had entered the police force as a way of making a name for himself. He rose through the force, and by the time he retired he had acquired an international reputation of which he was very proud. Injured in the First World War, he was obliged to seek refuge in England from the German occupation. Poirot had worked with Inspector Japp previously on the Abercrombie forgery case of 1904.

Hercule Poirot has an outstanding intellect, with the wisdom and experience which comes with age. Yet his physical appearance and peculiar characteristics mean that he is often underestimated until it is too late. Just over 5ft tall, 'with a luxurious black moustache, perfectly coifed black hair, piercing green eyes, and impeccable attire', he is obsessed with order and neatness. It is these physical and mental characteristics which help to make him so memorable.

Hercule Poirot was described as having a luxurious black moustache, perfectly coifed black hair and piercing green eyes. *Copyright Cathy Cook/Zowie Wyatt 2012.*

His obsession with symmetry includes displeasure at different size eggs! In *The ABC Murders* (1936) he rues the fact that science has not resolved the issue of hens laying eggs of different sizes. In *Peril at End House* (1932) he says that he cannot eat the eggs put before him as they are different sizes, and when asked in *Murder on the Orient Express* (1934) how he would like his eggs cooked, he says boiled but both exactly the same size. He is even teased by Inspector Japp in *Lord Edgware Dies* (1933) when Japp comments that Poirot has not got the hens to lay any square shaped eggs for him yet.

In *The Hollow* (1946) we are told that Poirot does not like trees as they have an untidy habit of shedding their leaves. However, it is his love of symmetry which allows him to find the vital clue in solving his first case in *The Mysterious Affair at Styles*.

Poirot has most of the characteristics that the British of the time were supposed to despise in bourgeois foreigners. He is vain, fussy, dapper and conceited enough to expect that everyone has heard of him and admires him. Yet it is vital that he is acceptable as a foreign hero to the readers. So although he has the veneer of a foreigner, he possesses the manners, social graces, values and sentiments so important to the British. His friendship with a proven British loyalist, Captain Hastings, also endorses his credibility.

However, he still seems a ridiculous character who does not command our instant respect, and murderers tend to underestimate him. Therefore, when he is proved to have been right all along, this makes it all the more impressive.

Christie hides Poirot's brilliance beneath a bizarre exterior and comic traits, allowing us to laugh at him occasionally, but respect him completely and be awed by his powers of deduction.

Agatha Christie used the Sherlock Holmes form of construction for her first detective, a brilliant detective with idiosyncrasies, supported in his role by a respectable but idiotic sidekick, Captain Hastings.

In some ways, Poirot was a reverse image of Christie herself – a short, confident, old Belgian bachelor of meticulousness neatness, created by a tall, shy, married, young Englishwoman renowned for her untidiness. A 1938 *Daily Mail* article by Agatha Christie also gave an interesting insight into this aspect of her writing. She said that if you are a person who is burdened with acute shyness and with only thinking of the correct thing to do or say when it is too late, then all you can do is write about quick-witted men and resourceful girls, whose reactions are like greased lightning.

After our first encounter with Hercule Poirot at Styles in 1920, he did not return to a war-torn Belgium, but instead moved to London. Initially he shared rooms at 14 Farraway Street with Captain Hastings. In 1926, Poirot decided to retire permanently and moved to Kings Abbott to grow marrows. However, the murder of Roger Ackroyd (1926) forced him back into detecting.

As the fees from his wealthy clients increased, he was able to adopt a more luxurious lifestyle. He moved to a chic flat at No 203 Whitehaven Mansions, London, a building which he greatly admired for its straight lines and symmetry. We learn that his telephone number was TRA(falgar) 8137 in *Dead Man's Folly* (1956).

Agatha does such an effective job at establishing his character in the early novels and short stories of the 1920s, that in future works he barely changes. Although she develops Poirot into a slightly more credible character in future adventures, she makes few changes, and it is interesting to note how little more we know of Poirot at the end of his long career than at the beginning. Over time however, as we follow his career, he becomes less eccentric in speech and appearance, and indeed seems to grow younger through some of his adventures; although as already mentioned, it has been estimated that he would be about 120 by the time of his last case!

By the time of his last case, *Curtain* (1975) he is showing his age, and when he returned to Styles, the place where it all began in 1920, he was suffering from arthritis and heart failure and spent most of his time in a wheelchair. However, nothing had dampened his little grey cells.

When Hercule Poirot died in 1975 he was buried at Styles St Mary (*Curtain* 1975), with no known heirs. He was the only fictional character up until then to have obituaries written for him in the newspapers. *The Daily Telegraph* had a whole column in its centre pages dedicated to their obituary.

The New York Times published a front-page obituary entitled 'Hercule Poirot is Dead: Famed Belgian Detective', saying that his career, as chronicled in the novels of Agatha Christie, was one of the most illustrious in fiction.

HERCULE POIROT'S PHYSICAL APPEARANCE

Physically, Poirot is as instantly recognisable as a cartoon character. Indeed, Agatha Christie most liked the image of him drawn for the serialisation of twelve short Poirot stories in *The Sketch* magazine in the spring of 1923. The illustration, drawn by W. Smithson Broadhead, shows a small sturdy man, with a haughty pose, dressed impeccably but with a disdainful expression. Agatha felt that this drawing was the closest she had seen to her own mental picture of him, showing him as short but not fat, extremely dapper, and with a very elegant moustache. Such was her disappointment with other images of her detective that soon afterwards she refused to let Poirot's image be included on any book covers.

In *The Mysterious Affair at Styles*, Hercule Poirot is described as 'an extraordinary-looking little man', little more than 5ft 4in tall. He has a head shaped exactly like an egg, although in later life Agatha confessed that she had no idea what an egg shaped head might be. His green eyes shine bright when he is excited.

Most famous perhaps of his psychical characteristics is his moustache. When we first meet him in 1920, his moustache

Artist's impression of Poirot, based on the drawing by W. Smithson Broadhead for *The Sketch* magazine. Agatha thought this image of Hercule Poirot was the closest to her own mental image of her detective. *Copyright Cathy Cook / Zowie Wyatt 2012.*

is described as very stiff and military. In *Murder in Mesopotamia* (1936) his moustache is described as 'enormous', and one character comments that he looks like 'a hairdresser in a comic play'.

In *After the Funeral* (1953) we are told that 'his moustache curved upwards in a flamboyant flourish', and in *Hickory Dickory Dock* (1955) Poirot has 'a moustache of ferocious proportions which he twirled contentedly'.

He is obsessed by his image, fussing about the neatness of his clothes and the exact symmetry of his hair parting. In *The ABC Murders* (1936) he admits to dyeing his hair and moustache, which is described elsewhere as 'suspiciously black'.

He wears striped trousers, black jacket and bow tie, as well as his famous patent leather shoes, and a muffler in colder weather. Early on his career, he carried a cane as he was recovering from an injury which caused him to limp.

HERCULE POIROT'S METHOD OF DETECTION

Both of Agatha Christie's main detectives, Miss Marple and Hercule Poirot, have the wisdom of experience and long life, but their methods of solving crimes are very different.

Poirot is always calm and collected, and reassures us that reason can solve any problem. His is a cerebral method of detection by 'using the little grey cells'. He looks down at the bloodhound Sherlock Holmes style of detective who rushes around searching for minute traces of incriminating evidence and measuring wet footprints in the grass, although he has been known to do the same thing himself on a couple of occasions.

Whereas the hands of the police are tied, Poirot has more scope to catch his criminal. Due to his past experience in the police force and the esteem in which he is held, Poirot wins the cooperation of Scotland Yard and is able to gain access to police files and information. His success as a private detective is because he is able to persuade the police to tell him what they know, and get them to respond to his suggestions and requests.

However, Poirot is not beyond secretly entering rooms with special pass keys and house-breaking to retrieve stolen or incriminating evidence. He will hire actors and stage phoney scenes to force confessions from murderers. Hastings however frowns on such activities, especially Poirot's listening at doors and opening other people's letters to gain evidence. Poirot also uses subterfuge when his brother Achille appears in *The Big Four* (1927), but of course nothing is what it seems.

In some circumstances, Poirot speaks with deliberately abominable English, convinced that Britain as a nation can be tricked into saying things if they think that there is only a foreigner around.

Poirot is most famous for his dénouement, the final re-enactment of the crime to reveal the murderer, with all of the suspects present. He will often highlight the most likely suspect and convince all those present that he has identified the murderer, only then to cleverly reverse and present a different but correct account of what happened and so expose the guilty person.

HERCULE POIROT'S PERSONAL LIFE

Gillian Gill, in her biography of Agatha Christie, sums up Poirot perfectly – as a retired man without a past, a single man without relatives, a man without lovers, a man without childhood friends, yet a man profoundly content with his life and destiny.

Hercule Poirot seems generally uninterested in sex, and as Martin Fido points out, the only supposed French characteristic that he singularly lacks is erotic charm or success. He has a mind whose pure logicality will never be distracted by his hormones. He can however be moved by great beauty, and he is a great lover of the arts and theatre.

He is cynical about romantic attachments, stating that 'women are never kind', although 'sometimes they can be tender' (*After the Funeral*, 1953). Perhaps unsurprisingly, he never marries, and is only ever linked romantically to one woman, the flamboyant Russian beauty Vera Rossakoff in *The Big Four* (1927). Rossakoff is often in his thoughts, and he compares the London girls he encounters in *One, Two, Buckle My Shoe* (1940) to her.

All of his life, Poirot only really has two close friends. Captain Hastings is his loyal sidekick and friend between 1920 and 1937, although he joins him again for his last case *Curtain* in 1975. Ariadne Oliver takes over this role between 1936 and 1973 and becomes his assistant in those situations requiring an insider of social events and circles. Their partnership works well, with often comic effect. He also has friendships through work, with both Inspector Japp and Superintendent Battle.

When Poirot initially plans to retire in 1926, he chooses to do so to the country, and it is at Kings Abbott where, growing marrows in his garden, he gets involved in *The Murder of Roger Ackroyd*. Returning to his detecting career, he often treats himself to holidays abroad, or escapes for a weekend to the country in a rented cottage, as we learn in *The Hollow* (1946).

However even on holiday, Poirot finds himself involved in murders, and from the 1940s the number of his foreign adventures reduces both in amount and geographical range. He tends to stay at his London apartment and have clients come and visit him by appointment.

As for culinary tastes, he enjoys a breakfast of brioche, an occasional croissant and hot chocolate (*Third Girl*, 1966), and is very content to eat a well-prepared omelette when at home. Poirot drinks 'tisanes instead of tea, *sirop de cassis* (blackcurrant syrup) instead of whisky, and drinking chocolate instead of coffee', according to Martin Fido.

He considers himself to be a gourmet, and as his income increases with each solved case, he frequents the Savoy and the Ritz, as well as French restaurants in Soho, as often as he pleases. He is a lover of French *cordon bleu* cuisine, and avoids English tearooms and ordinary village cafes.

HERCULE POIROT'S RENOWN

Hercule Poirot is egotism personified. He freely admits that he is a great man. He is not however infallible. The only failure in his career occurred during his early years in the Belgian police force, and is documented in the short story, 'The Chocolate Box' (1924). In it Poirot reveals how he almost sent an innocent man to the guillotine. He instructed Hastings to whisper 'chocolate box' in his ear if he ever became too conceited about his abilities. (Interestingly, Sherlock Holmes requests Watson whisper 'Norbury' in his ear for a similar reason!)

Despite this though, he is conceited enough to expect the whole world to have heard about him, and admire him. Indeed, his fame as a detective has travelled widely, and there are several instances where his reputation preceded him. For example, in *Death in the Clouds* (1935) Monsieur Fournier of the French Sûreté had heard of him from the inspector in charge of the case in *Murder on the Links* (1923).

Proud of his reputation, he is most put-out when people do not recognise his name, which happens more frequently as he gets older. He consciously stops himself from saying that most people have heard of him when he realises that most of them are now probably lying in graveyards (*Elephants Can Remember*, 1972).

Hercule Poirot's reputation means that he can charge very high professional fees when circumstances allow. In 1934's *Murder on the Orient Express*, Poirot is offered and declines

Hercule Poirot, Agatha's famous Belgian detective, is immortalised as a statue in Ellezelles, Belgium.

$20,000 to protect Mr Ratchett (estimated at approximately $325,000 today). He becomes so wealthy from his fees that he considers retiring again as early as *The Mystery of the Blue Train* (1928), and Inspector Japp is often amazed at the financial success he has made of his detective business.

Poirot is just as willing to take cases from members of the lower classes, although he prefers to work for the higher echelons of society, and will readily mention the work he has done for royalty and foreign governments.

POIROT AS VIEWED BY HIS CREATOR AND ACTORS WHO HAVE PLAYED HIM

Hercule Poirot thrived under Agatha Christie's pen for more than fifty-five years until his demise in 1975. She mastered a convincing masculine voice in her writing, but understandably, Agatha herself tired of him. However, Poirot had so endeared himself to the readers and publishers that she was not allowed, due to public demand, to abandon him.

In a 1938 article in the *Daily Mail*, Agatha said that there had been moments when she has wondered why she ever invented this 'detestable, bombastic, tiresome little creature'. At other times she admitted to finding him insufferable, but like most public men they don't like retiring, and that Poirot wouldn't either all the while that he was her main source of income. As the years went by though, she said that she held off introducing Poirot until as late as she feasibly could in the story.

The 1938 *Daily Mail* article was a major insight into her views of Poirot, as Agatha Christie wrote the whole piece herself. She explained how she first developed her character, and how, from a rough outline of external characteristics, certain personality traits seemed to automatically follow. For example, because he was a small dandified man, she felt he would be conceited and meticulous. She said that there was more to him than she ever expected there would be at the start, in particular his intense interest in the psychology of murder, and the fact that every crime had a definite signature.

Agatha admitted in the article that there were moments when she had intensely hated Hercule Poirot, and had rebelled bitterly against being chained to him for life. But over time, he had won, and that she now had a reluctant affection for him as he had become more human and less irritating. She finished the article by saying that even though she was beholden to him financially, they were foremost friends and partners.

So what did the actors who played the great detective think of him?

Peter Ustinov played Hercule Poirot for EMI's second and third films, *Death on the Nile* in 1978, and *Evil Under the Sun* in 1982. He described Poirot as 'terribly accurate', meticulous, and 'tidy in his mind and habits', but he said that he should have 'hated to know him, as he was so vain, self-contained and finicky'.

Ustinov admitted that he had never read a detective story, let alone any of Agatha Christie's books, before taking on the role of Poirot. He joked that there was never a chance of him giving the solution away during filming, as although he had read the script he could never remember who the murderer was. Ustinov developed a genuine Belgian accent for Poirot by listening to the Belgian Ambassador to Paris. He noticed how he did not drop his 'h's but instead would add them where they are not supposed to be. Poirot would, therefore, pronounce alibi as 'halibi'.

David Suchet is the television personification of Hercule Poirot that most people now recognise. He started off playing Inspector Japp in the TV film version of *Lord Edgware Dies*, called *Thirteen for Dinner*, in 1985, but was offered the role of Poirot in 1989. LWT decided to set all the episodes in 1935 rather than range across the years as the original stories do.

Suchet describes Hercule Poirot as a 'walking brain', irritating, insufferable, egotistic and pompous, but also a man of 'enormous charm'. In order to perfect Poirot's accent and mannerisms, Suchet stays in character at all times when on set, even during lunch. He said that if he had to keep going in and out of the voice, it would add up to an hour onto his day.

His aim is to portray Poirot exactly as Agatha Christie intended, and so he has read every single book and short story and made copious notes, some of which he carries with him on set. He said that his wife prefers living with him when he is playing Poirot as he is so much tidier as a result!

John Moffatt is the voice of Hercule Poirot in BBC Radio Four's adaptations of the Poirot stories. He has a special pair of tight leather shoes which he wears when recording the radio drama, as the tightness makes his feet feel small, and so he feels in the character of a neat little man, twirling his imaginary moustache. Although scenes are often recorded out of sequence, for the Poirot stories the final recording is always where Poirot does his dénouement. Moffat comes dressed in a suit, in his tight shoes, and stands opposite all of the cast members who are arranged as if they were in front of

Poirot as he reveals who the murderer is. This apparently has an amazing psychological effect upon the cast, because faced with John Moffatt as Poirot, he 'plays' the cast, lifting his eyes up as he addresses each cast member in turn, and even those actors who know it is not them, are made to feel guilty!

• Miss Jane Marple •

Appearing in twelve novels and twenty short stories, Miss Jane Marple first appeared in a series of six short stories published in the *Royal Magazine* from December 1927. These later formed the basis of *The Thirteen Problems* (1932), but her first major appearance in a full length novel was in *Murder at the Vicarage* (1930). It would be over a decade before she solved another murder in *The Body in the Library* (1942). As Agatha herself reached her 60s, the frequency with which her elderly female detective was called upon to solve her cases increased.

Born in about the 1850s, we first meet Miss Marple when she is, according to Agatha, between about 65 and 70. Miss Marple is described as an English girl 'from a Cathedral Close' and probably, therefore, the daughter of a canon or dean of a cathedral. Two of her uncles were also canons of cathedrals – Uncle Thomas was a Canon of Ely, and another uncle was Canon of Chichester Cathedral.

Like her creator, she was educated at home, in this case by a German governess, and then studied abroad as a teenager at a finishing school, in Miss Marple's case in Florence. Her sister married and was the mother of Miss Marple's nephew Raymond West, who writes modern novels and modern poetry 'with no capital letters'.

Miss Marple herself never married, although she did have several suitors – one of whom was suitable but very dull, and the relationship of another was nipped in the bud by her mother, for which she was later very grateful when she met the man again and he was 'really quite dreadful'.

Miss Marple lives alone in the village of St Mary Mead where she has lived for over fifty years. St Mary Mead is in the county of Downshire (occasionally Radfordshire), and is about 25 miles south of London, about 12 miles from Market Basing, and also 12 miles from the coast. Anne Hart points out that it is not the same St Mary Mead which is mentioned in *The Mystery of the Blue Train* (1928) as this village was in Kent.

Agatha Christie gives a complete and full description of the village, its High Street, its residents, and so creates a believable and totally self-contained environment in which many of the Miss Marple stories are set. It is also her role within the community which helps to define Miss Marple, and the fact that she is readily accepted allows her to play a key role in solving the crimes within the village.

During the final years of her career, Miss Marple does a surprising amount of travelling, including holidays to the Caribbean and tours around the UK. She is a credible character, and her common-sense values give her universal appeal.

MISS JANE MARPLE'S PHYSICAL APPEARANCE

In the short stories within *The Thirteen Problems*, Miss Marple wears black, with black lace gloves and a black lace cap on top of her 'piled up masses of snowy white hair'. By the time of her appearance in her first full length novel, Miss Marple has toned down her style and is a less severe-looking white-haired old lady with a 'gentle and appealing manner', 'deceptively fragile', but 'uncommonly shrewd'.

She is tall and thin, with pink cheeks and pretty 'china blue eyes', which can look innocent or shrewd depending on the circumstances. She is described as having a 'gentle, rather fussy manner', and has also been described as 'inconsequential'. Due to the very fact that she is gentle, elderly and very 'proper', she appears benign and a threat to no one. Indeed, people will tend to overlook her, and so let their guard down, giving her all the evidence she is looking for.

MISS JANE MARPLE'S METHOD OF DETECTION

Miss Marple's hobbies of bird watching, gardening and gossiping, all allow her to carry out the subtle observation of the goings on within the village. Often more eager to watch people rather than birds with her binoculars, her gardening too is more of a cover to allow her to keep an eye on things. In later books though she becomes much less of a snoop, relying more on insight than binoculars. Gossip is of course a socially useful activity, and vital to any detective operating in a tight-knit community!

Her role as an amateur sleuth began in the late 1920s when she used to invite a group of friends for dinner at her home every Tuesday night, and they would present detective puzzles to be solved by the rest of the group, such as the theft of the Church Boys' Outing Money.

Whilst Miss Marple's experience of life is neither wide nor deep, she has spent a lifetime observing the goings on in St Mary Mead. She does not trust people and always expects the worst. A shrewd observer, she solves crime by analogy, seeking parallels between current and past crimes, perceiving similarities in human behaviours and believing that human nature never changes. She sees St Mary Mead as a microcosm of the world.

Her keen understanding of human nature, often guided by feminine intuition, is reinforced by a strong sense of morals and values. She has a powerful capacity for deductive logic. Yet all the while she portrays a character of frailty and fluffiness, who is muddled, timid and unworldly. The contradictory elements of her character work to maximum effect. She apparently just happens to find herself in the vicinity of murder more often than most!

It is interesting that Miss Marple was not given any particular 'Watson' or companion, unlike Poirot. She does however have an entourage of assistants and helpers, including several policemen who prove invaluable.

Miss Marple's mission is to expose the murderer, rather than to ensure their arrest. Quite often it is the guilt of the act which causes the murderer to confess! Her favourite sayings are 'beware of first impressions' and 'nothing is ever as it seems'.

VIEWS OF MISS MARPLE BY HER CREATOR AND ACTRESSES WHO HAVE PLAYED HER

Agatha Christie's view was that Miss Marple was at her best when solving problems in short stories, so *The Thirteen Problems* (1932) were, for Agatha, the real essence of Miss Marple. She much preferred Miss Marple to Hercule Poirot.

In creating Miss Marple, Agatha achieved something quite unprecedented – a second character of equal success as Hercule Poirot.

In her autobiography, Christie was quite clear that Miss Marple was not a picture of her grandmother. However, she did share the trait of always expecting the worst of everything and everyone. Agatha said that Grannie could apparently spot a 'wrong-un' a mile off, because the person would remind her of deviant characters she had met in the past. Agatha endowed Miss Marple with Grannie's powers of intuition and prophecy.

Barbara Mullen was the first actress to play Miss Marple, when in 1949 she portrayed the character in a stage adaptation of *Murder at the Vicarage*. Prior to her death in 1979, she said that since then she had time to study all of Miss Marple's idiosyncrasies. She now saw her as a 'gentlewoman' with a subtle sense of humour, but 'believing absolutely in good and evi', and fighting evil as an 'avenging fury'.

Joan Hickson said that she adored and admired the character of Miss Marple. She considered her a 'wonderful woman with very high standards', very strong-minded, with a 'clear outlook on life'. Joan Hickson played Miss Marple in the first of the BBC television serialisations from 1984, and admitted that her famous pondering look was not all it seemed – that thoughtful, faraway look as Miss Marple coolly solves a murder, was usually Ms Hickson wondering what was for lunch! When she was awarded an OBE in 1987, the Queen said it was for Miss Marple, as she had liked the series very much.

• Tommy & Tuppence Beresford •

Featuring in four novels and sixteen short stories, the Beresfords were created in Agatha's second book *The Secret Adversary* (1922) and appeared in the very last book to be written by Agatha, *Postern of Fate* (1973). (The final stories of Hercule Poirot and Miss Marple were actually written during the Second World War.) Her lifelong devotion to the Beresfords show how they held a place in her heart.

Tommy Beresford was born in 1894 in Suffolk. There was a strong hint of some shadow hovering over his birth, and no father was ever mentioned. Physically he is typically British, with 'exquisitely slicked-back' red hair, which turns sandy-grey with age. He has a nondescript, but 'pleasantly ugly' face, 'unmistakably the face of a gentleman'. His height and weight are apparently inconsequential.

Tuppence Cowley, destined to become Mrs Beresford, has a 'vigorous curling mop' of black hair, a 'determined chin and large wide apart grey eyes'. Whilst Tuppence has 'no claim to beauty', her elfin face radiates both character and charm.

She is fifth daughter of Archdeacon Cowley of Little Missendell in Suffolk. She is said to be a similar age to Tommy, but in the last novel he is over 70 and she is 66. Tuppence has at least four sisters, and like many of Agatha's young detectives, she comes from a well-educated family.

When Tommy and Tuppence meet again for the first time since childhood, he is an army lieutenant who has seen military action in France, and Tuppence is a maid-of-all-work in a London officers' hospital. They meet at Dover Street Underground station, which no longer exists.

In terms of character, Tommy is careful and reasoned, whereas Tuppence is impetuous and volatile. Their one time boss, Mr Carter, describes Tommy as a rather 'block-headed' young man, 'slow in his mental processes', but it is impossible to lead him astray or deceive him as he doesn't have any imagination.

Tuppence, with her more vibrant and ebullient personality, has less common sense and relies more on intuition. Together they complement each other, Tommy using his deduction while Tuppence uses her intuition, but both acting with pace and stamina.

Initially setting up their own agency as 'adventurers for hire' in *The Secret Adversary* (1922), by *Partners in Crime* (1929) they have been married six years, and Tommy is working in the administration department of the secret service.

Twelve years later, in *N or M?*, the Beresfords have twins – Deborah is in the code-breaking department of British Intelligence and Derek is in the RAF. They have also adopted a child called Betty, who later takes up government work in South Africa. By the time of *By the Pricking of My Thumbs* (1968), Tommy and Tuppence's daughter Deborah has three children, making Tommy and Tuppence proud grandparents.

As the novels follow the Beresfords throughout their life, from their youth in *The Secret Adversary* (1922) to retirement in *Postern of Fate* (1973), they become increasingly more credible, as Agatha continues to develop and build on their characters. Initially Tuppence's naive eagerness to go on dangerous assignments seem unreal, but as she gets older, she becomes in many ways a more interesting character, less reliant on Tommy, and with her own sense of fearless resourcefulness.

Their adventures are amongst the most light-hearted in Agatha's novels. From the very start of her writing career, Christie liked to intersperse her complicated detective stories with easier to write thrillers or adventure stories.

In the Beresfords' second book, *Partners in Crime*, it provides a compendium of what Agatha Christie herself had read, as each short story revolves around Tommy and Tuppence solving crimes, whilst mimicking the methods of other famous literary detectives, such as Father Brown. Agatha proves her skill at satire and parody, gently poking fun at her fellow authors, and even at her own detective Hercule Poirot in the last chapter.

The fame and world renown of Hercule Poirot and Miss Marple tend to overshadow Christie's young detecting pair. However, the first ever British radio serialisation of an Agatha Christie book was of *Partners in Crime*, broadcast every Monday night for thirteen weeks starting in April 1953. Richard Attenborough and his wife Sheila Sim played the characters of Tommy and Tuppence.

• CAPTAIN ARTHUR HASTINGS •

Captain Arthur Hastings originally met Poirot whilst working for Lloyds of London on a business trip to Belgium. During the First World War he was wounded in the Somme and was invalided out of the army. We first meet him in Agatha's initial book, *The Mysterious Affair at Styles* (1920). In the manner of Arthur Conan Doyle's Sherlock Holmes, Agatha used a narrator who was the detective's best friend for her stories, acting as the reader's substitute on the scene.

As a complete opposite to the eccentric Belgian detective Poirot, Hastings is the model of British convention and propriety, with an honourable war record. He is respectable and nice, but also idiotic and stupid. He admires pretty girls, especially redheads, and he himself has a small 'toothbrush' moustache. However, it is not apparent why Poirot should have such a close

friendship with someone who has such a contrasting character to his own – a very odd couple!

Educated at Eton, Hastings is working as a private secretary for an MP by the time of the second Poirot novel,
Murder on the Links (1923). However, Agatha then married
Captain Hastings off, and he emigrated with his wife, Dulcie
Duveen who was almost twenty years his junior, to a ranch
in Argentina. He conveniently returns for occasional adventures with Poirot, and in *The ABC Murders* (1936) he returns
to Britain for six months to collect an OBE and sort out his
business affairs.

He has a thirty-year happy marriage until his wife's death,
and they have four children together, two sons and two daughters. One of his daughters, Judith, appears in the last Poirot
novel, *Curtain* (1975).

• ARIADNE OLIVER •

Appearing in eight novels, Ariadne Oliver always seems to hold
the key to the mystery, but doesn't solve it herself. She will usually involve herself in a case to oblige a frantic friend.

Mrs Oliver makes her first appearance in a short story
in *Parker Pyne Investigates* (1934). By this stage, as a world-
famous novelist, she has already produced forty-six novels,
all of them bestsellers in England and America. Her main
creation is a Finnish detective called Sven Hjerson. Her for-
mula for a successful detective story is plenty of dead bodies,

the cover-up murder of a key witness, and untraceable poisons. Through her experience as an author, she becomes invaluable to Poirot in helping him solve the murders she becomes embroiled in.

She is a widow of 'middle age, handsome in an untidy fashion, with fine eyes' and a 'large quantity of rebellious grey hair'. She works surrounded by untidy piles of papers and a bag of apples, just like her creator. As she writes her books, she will wander around the room mouthing dialogue to herself and pulling at her hair. She hates politics, drinks *crème de menthe* and *kirsch*, and never knows what to say to fans she meets.

Poirot turns out to be an avid reader of Mrs Oliver's detective novels, and she becomes a sounding board for Poirot's ideas. She fulfils the role of amateur sleuth herself, as well as being a friend and helper to Poirot as he solves the murders. Such was Poirot's affection for Ariadne Oliver that she is the only adult, apart from servants, that Poirot ever addressed by her first name.

By *Mrs McGinty's Dead* (1952), Mrs Oliver has become an undisguised self-caricature of Agatha Christie – a disorganised, overweight, aging detective story writer. On one occasion, Poirot is called upon to extricate her from a small two-seater car which is too small and inappropriate for someone of her age. For anyone reading Agatha's own autobiography, the themes are very familiar!

• PARKER PYNE •

In 1934, Agatha Christie published the collection of stories called *Parker Pyne Investigates* (1934). Appearing in a total of fourteen short stories, Parker Pyne is in his 60s, bald and large but not fat, with little twinkling eyes behind strong glasses. He is a retired civil servant who has spent thirty-five years compiling statistics for the government. He is the son of Charles and Harriet Parker Pyne, and his first name is James in the first few stories, although he signs his first name as Christopher in a hotel register in a later story, perhaps as a pseudonym.

Details of his background, character and lifestyle are limited, as the focus of the short stories is more on plot, rather than on development of characters.

Parker Pyne is a wise elderly observer. He advertises in newspapers with a personal ad which asks:

Are you happy? If not, consult Mr Parker Pyne, 17 Richmond Street.

In the first few short stories, he claims to know the five causes of human unhappiness, only two of which are disclosed – boredom and sexual jealously. He constructs elaborate scenarios and charades, plays theatrical games and uses actors to help resolve the issue or problem which is causing the client their unhappiness.

• HARLEY QUIN •

Harley Quin is a mysterious almost supernatural and spiritual character, appearing and then disappearing unexpectedly in fourteen short stories. Like a Harlequin figure, strange tricks of the light caused by stained glass or flickering firelight make his clothes appear multi-coloured. Working with the elderly Mr Satterthwaite, they appear whenever crime threatens the happiness of lovers, averting marital disasters and reuniting estranged partners. Quin helps his colleague solve various puzzles by injecting into the situation exactly what Satterthwaite needs to reach the right conclusion, by prodding and guiding, asking pertinent questions, and acting as a catalyst.

When Mr Satterthwaite first meets Harley Quin he is so charmed and excited by the harlequin's powers, that a totally new aspect of his character develops – instead of remaining on the side-lines just observing, he becomes more assertive, more involved with people and their problems, more in touch with life and the human spirit.

The *Mysterious Mr Quin* published in 1930 was one of Agatha's favourite collection of short stories. The stories fused the mystery puzzle of detective novels with the romance and fantasy of fairy tales. Agatha herself described Harley Quin as a friend of lovers, but connected with death. Death is prevalent in these short stories, with suicide often as a result of the loss of love.

• CHIEF INSPECTOR JAPP •

Chief Inspector James Japp of Scotland Yard appears in sixteen Poirot novels and twelve short stories. All detective stories need policemen, but Agatha ensures that her policemen are human beings, with characters, personalities and family backgrounds.

Chief Inspector Japp is the most long-suffering of Christie's characters, following in Poirot's wake, always one step behind, as Lestrade did to Sherlock Holmes. However, here Agatha created a strong friendship and respect between the two.

Poirot first worked with Japp on a case in Brussels in 1904. Having worked his way up through the ranks, Japp initially appears in the first Christie book, *The Mysterious Affair at Styles* (1920) as a somewhat ludicrous character, over eager, unattractive ('a little sharp, dark, ferret-faced man'), and lower middle class. As we see him accompany Poirot along his career, he becomes more articulate with experience and age.

Japp emerges as an outstanding policeman, with increased stature, performance and reputation. Similarly, these changes are reflected in the attitudes of Poirot and Hastings. Hastings is initially very resentful and contemptuous of Japp but this changes into a relationship of respect for the chief inspector.

Very much at the beck and call of his respected friend Poirot, Japp has been known to say:

I don't know why I bother sometimes. I may as well stay at home and do my garden. Who do you want me to arrest now Poirot?

4

KEY WORKS

IT IS HARD TO highlight just a few key works from an author who is said to have sold more books than Shakespeare and the Bible. However, without doubt, *The Mousetrap* deserves a mention because of its record-breaking status, and in terms of her novels, the most stunningly original plots are those in *The Murder of Roger Ackroyd* and *And Then There Were None*.

Agatha herself always found it hard to explain how she created her plots. As G.C. Ramsey pointed out, it is hard for any naturally talented person to explain how they come by their talent, so a musician with perfect pitch can recognise a note, but will find it almost impossible to explain just why or how he can recognise and identify the sound so easily. Nevertheless, that Agatha had natural talent is unquestionable, given the success of her works.

• THE MOUSETRAP •

The longest continuously running play in the world, according to the *Guinness Book of Records*, *The Mousetrap* has been playing in London since before Queen Elizabeth II came to the throne. Its first performance in 1952 was at a time when Sir Winston Churchill was the Prime Minister of England, Harry S. Truman was President of the USA, and Joseph Stalin was running the USSR.

The Mousetrap originated as a thirty-minute radio play entitled *Three Blind Mice*, written in 1946 at the special request of the BBC. The Director General of the BBC wrote to Queen

St Martin's Theatre is located in West Street, Cambridge Circus, London.

Mary in 1946, offering her an evening of her favourite pro-
grammes to commemorate her 80th birthday. Her private
secretary wrote back saying that she would like to celebrate
by listening to a new Agatha Christie play, as well as music by
the BBC Theatre Orchestra and A Gala Variety Show.

Agatha, who was always a huge fan of the royal family, was
thrilled and set about creating a classic whodunit. She asked
that her initial fee for the commission go to the Southport
Infirmary Children's Toy Fund.

Although taking its name from the famous nursery rhyme,
the plot was based on a real-life case. She remembered an idea
that had come to her when reading about the dreadful murder
of Dennis O'Neill, and developed this into a play.

The radio play took Agatha just one week to write. Broadcast
on Friday, 30 May 1947, it was listened to by Queen Mary in
the sitting room of Marlborough House, where she was cel-
ebrating her birthday with friends and family. It proved a very
satisfactory present and Her Majesty was simply delighted.

Shortly afterwards, Agatha Christie turned the radio play
into a short story which was published in *Cosmopolitan* magazine in America, and then as part of a collection *Three Blind
Mice and Other Stories* (1950) again in America only.

Five years later, in 1951, Agatha decided to expand the
radio drama into a three-act play. In her autobiography she
said that she felt it would work well as a three-act thriller,
with the addition of some extra characters, a fuller plot and
background, and a slower build to the climax.

Three Blind Mice opened in a pre-London showing at the Theatre Royal in Nottingham on Monday, 6 October 1952. It then toured to Oxford, Manchester, Liverpool, Newcastle, Leeds and Birmingham before reaching London's West End in November. However, during this time the audiences' lukewarm reception led to extensive re-writing of the script before the opening night in London.

Agatha realised that it was neither a thriller, nor a comedy-thriller, so she sat up all night with the producer, Peter Saunders, removing jokes which detracted from the tension and mystery. The original version had two set changes and ten characters, but by the opening night it had just a single set and two fewer characters.

However, a change of name was required because there already existed a play named *Three Blind Mice*. Agatha's son-in-law suggested the name of *The Mousetrap*, which appears as the title of a play that Hamlet had intended to write but never got around to, as mentioned in *Hamlet*, Act III, Scene Two.

The Mousetrap opened at London's Ambassadors Theatre on 25 November 1952, with Peter Saunders predicting a twelve-month run, and Agatha saying that it wouldn't run for that long, maybe eight months at the most.

Richard Attenborough initially played the role of Detective Sergeant Trotter, the policeman who arrives at a snowbound guesthouse to warn visitors that there is a killer amongst them. His wife Sheila Sim also starred in the opening cast list. Though Agatha had been sure that Sheila Sim was right for the role of the pretty young wife, oddly enough she was less certain about Richard Attenborough in the role of the policeman.

On 23 March 1974, *The Mousetrap* finished its twenty-one-year run at the Ambassador's Theatre and transferred the following Monday to the slightly larger theatre next door, the St Martin's Theatre, without a break in the continuity of the run. It has continued to play at St Martin's Theatre ever since, without interruption.

⁓

There has been much debate about the reasons for the success and longevity of *The Mousetrap*. A large part of this is as a result of producer Peter Saunders' successful marketing. When audience numbers started to drop, he noisily celebrated its 1,000th performance with a party at the Savoy Hotel in London on 24 April 1955. Referred to by the press as 'A Night of a Thousand Stars', Agatha personally greeted every guest.

Another key to *The Mousetrap*'s long-running success is, as Agatha's husband Max pointed out, the natural genius of the author. Agatha's own view was that it was the sort of light play that you can take anyone to, including children and old ladies. It is not really frightening or horrible, even though there are elements of this within it, and because it is well-constructed, it manages to keep the interest of the audience to the end.

In addition, the small theatre size with a capacity of just 550 means that running costs and overheads are low, and once the play caught on, it became part of the tourist trail, as important as seeing Buckingham Palace and the Tower of London.

Each anniversary of *The Mousetrap* was celebrated with a hugely publicised party, to which famous stars and even royalty were invited. The press loved them and the resultant publicity reflected well on the popularity of Agatha's other books.

When the play became the longest-running play in the history of British theatre with its 2,239th performance, yet another spectacular party was held at the Savoy. Peter Saunders asked Agatha to arrive early so as to avoid the press; however, as she approached the banquet hall, a porter who did not recognise the guest of honour told her that it would be another twenty minutes before anyone was allowed in. In her autobiography she remembers the frustration at her own shyness, the fact that she couldn't explain who she was and just turned and walked away. She said that she felt like a fraud, and that even thinking back on the day all those years ago, she still felt like she spent her life *pretending* to be an author.

In 1972, after twenty years of running, Peter Saunders gave yet another one of his thousand star parties. There were doubts as to whether Agatha, then in her 80s, would be able to come, having recently suffered from a broken hip. In the event, she appeared for the party looking frail and wearing carpet slippers. However, as she arrived she told Peter Saunders that she had left her teeth at home, and as there was no time to go and fetch them, it was agreed that only very intimate friends were allowed to speak to her as she didn't want to open her mouth!

When asked on her 80th birthday by the *Daily Mail* whether *The Mousetrap* was her favourite, she replied that it wasn't, as that was *The Crooked House*. However, she said that even though they changed the cast of *The Mousetrap* every year to prevent staleness, there was one character that they had never succeeded in casting exactly right yet – but she would not be drawn on which character that was, and it still remains a mystery.

The film rights were sold to Romulus Films and producer Victor Saville, in 1956, on the condition that any film must not appear until six months after the end of the stage run. Though Peter Saunders asked twice if he could buy back the rights, Mr Saville refused to sell, saying he was prepared to sit back and wait, as he believed he had a gold mine. Unfortunately, Victor Saville was outrun by the play and he died in 1979.

The rights and royalties to *The Mousetrap* were given to Mathew Prichard around his ninth birthday. However, he then sold his rights to *The Mousetrap* to Peter Saunders who continued to make a fortune from the run, until he retired from active management, selling them on to the play's then producer Stephen Waley-Cohen.

One of the nicest stories surrounding *The Mousetrap* is told by Riley & McAllister, about fan Pam Burford, who probably holds the record for the number of times she saw the play – over 140 times, and all during the initial two-year period that

Richard Attenborough was acting in it. After he left the cast she did not see *The Mousetrap* again. When Peter Saunders saw her outside the stage door of another play in which Attenborough was appearing, he asked her how many times she had seen that play. 'Only once', she replied, 'I don't like the play!'

• *THE MURDER OF ROGER ACKROYD* •

It is very hard to discuss the controversial plot device with which Agatha Christie's novel, *The Murder of Roger Ackroyd* (1926), established her reputation and sales without revealing the solution. If you haven't read the book, you should, because it was revolutionary within the field of crime fiction at the time. Therefore, please excuse any vagueness with regards to the plot device in the section which follows.

Both Agatha's brother-in-law, James, and Lord Louis Mountbatten, claim to have offered the plot solution which formed the basis of Agatha's most famous novel. Mountbatten, the uncle of Prince Philip, tells how he boasted to his daughters later in life that he gave Agatha the plot to her best book, and when asked to prove it, he couldn't. So he wrote to Agatha in 1969, asking for some proof. According to Gwen Robyns, Agatha wrote back saying she was very grateful to him for writing, as it had been playing on her conscience and she could now acknowledge the origin of the plot. She also said that she had once stood next to him at a cocktail party and had wanted to say who she was, and did he remember suggesting the plot, but she had been too shy. By the next post, Lord Mountbatten received a copy of the book, *The Murder of Roger Ackroyd*, with an inscription which said it was in grateful remembrance of a letter he wrote forty-five years ago which contained the suggestion that she then used in the book.

Julian Symonds described *The Murder of Roger Ackroyd* as the best shock ending of all time. Agatha Christie always maintained that she had played fair, and hadn't broken any rules of crime fiction. No false words were uttered, she said, and it was not unfair to leave things out when it is clear to the careful reader that a period of time has been unaccounted for. But the outcry by the press and critics was long and loud, and she was accused of an unscrupulous use of the least-likely-person motive.

However, the uproar did not in any way hurt the book's success, and from 1926 her sales rose steadily and never looked back.

• *AND THEN THERE WERE NONE* •

Agatha Christie's fame as a playwright was assured when she adapted her extraordinary novel of *Ten Little Niggers* (1939) into a play. The book has understandably since been renamed as *Ten Little Indians*, *And Then There Were None*, and *The Nursery Rhyme Murders*.

Agatha had taken such great care in writing the original book, that when the opportunity came up to transfer it to the stage, she decided that she would take on the challenge of making it work in the theatre.

Based on a famous nursery rhyme, the story tells the tale of what happened to the ten little Indians who one by one are murdered by various means and methods. The origin of the rhyme is said to date back to American Septimus Winner in 1864, and was adapted in England by Frank Green in 1868-69. Agatha wrote that the ending in her childhood days had been, 'he got married, and then there were none', but the original ending was apparently 'he went and hanged himself' and then there were none. She therefore used one in the novel, and the other in her stage play version. Such was her skills that both endings are convincing.

However, those to whom the script was first shown thought that the audiences would fall about laughing at such a plethora of corpses. Several promoters turned the play down before Betram Meyer finally decided to take a chance with it.

It opened at the St James' Theatre in November 1943, where it played for 260 performances, until a German bomb forced the theatre to close, and it moved to the Cambridge Theatre. In 1944 the play went to New York, renamed *Ten Little Indians*, and in 1966 the play was similarly retitled in the Britain.

In December 1947, the BBC initiated what was to become an almost annual event, the 'Christie for Christmas' radio play. The first 'Christie for Christmas' was a ninety-minute radio adaptation of the stage play, *Ten Little Indians*. The film version, called *And Then There Were None*, had previously been made by French director Rene Clair in 1945. It, therefore, became the first of Agatha's works to appear in all four entertainment media (stage, film, radio and television) when it was adapted for BBC TV in 1949.

A poll on the Christie Mystery website, although unscientific, shows the esteem with which *And Then There Were None* is held. When asked to vote for their favourite Agatha Christie, 21 per cent voted for *And Then There Were None*. The second highest vote went to *The Murder of Roger Ackroyd* at just 7 per cent.

• *MURDER ON THE ORIENT EXPRESS* •

First published in 1934, *Murder on the Orient Express* caused quite a sensation due to its unusual ending. Agatha took her inspiration from the real-life kidnapping of the Lindbergh baby, and also the marooning of the Orient Express in a snowdrift in 1929, when it was cut off from the rest of the world for six days.

From this she developed a murder mystery in a closed, almost claustrophobic, environment where the murderer *has* to be one of the limited number of suspects. No one is able to enter or leave the train due to the paralysing blizzard which has drawn the Orient Express to a halt. Hercule Poirot also takes justice into his own hands and controversially does not tell the police the full story after his dénouement.

The Orient Express train had always held a special place in Agatha's heart. Following the breakdown of her first marriage, Agatha went on a solo trip to Baghdad, travelling on the Orient Express, having heard of Leonard Woolley's archaeological discoveries which were being talked up as the second Tutankhamen. She also spent part of her honeymoon with Max on the train, and they would subsequently travel on the Orient Express on their yearly expeditions to Nimrud.

Murder on the Orient Express was dedicated to her husband Max. As one would expect in a Christie novel, the opulence of the train receives only minimal commentary, with the focal point as always being on plot and characters.

However, it was the decision to allow the novel to be turned into a film that propelled Agatha's fame even further. The film attracted almost cult status, was a huge box office success, and introduced Agatha Christie to a new audience.

After the disastrous MGM movies starring Margaret Rutherford as Miss Marple in the early 1960s, Agatha had sworn that she would never again allow her books to be made into movies. When MGM proposed to write a screenplay of *Murder on the Orient Express*, but with Miss Marple substituting Hercule Poirot, Agatha was adamantly against it. She told her agent that the book had taken a lot of careful planning, and to have it 'transformed into a rollicking farce with Miss Marple injected into it and probably in the role of the engine driver, though great fun', would be harmful to her reputation. She refused to sell any more film rights to MGM.

In the 1970s, Lord Mountbatten's son-in-law, Lord Brabourne, who was a successful independent film producer, got the backing of the giant EMI Corporation, to see if they could persuade Christie to let them make the film of *Murder on the Orient Express*. Brabourne had recently produced the film, *The Tales of Beatrix Potter* with the Royal Ballet Company, and Agatha had been a big fan of the film.

Over lunch with the author, they explained that they had located an authentic Orient Express coach in France, and they were bringing it back to England to rebuild it and lovingly recreate the atmosphere of the original. They planned an international cast list, and intended to stay very loyal and faithful to the original book.

The film took just forty-two days to shoot, and most of the location work took place in France and Turkey, with the Orient Express coach restored at Elstree Studios. In France, the film crew prayed for snow which was so essential to the plot, and the night before the scheduled start of shooting, snow fell thickly, making the Orient Express truly snowbound for the relevant scenes.

Prior to its distribution, a private showing of *Murder on the Orient Express* was given to Agatha Christie and her family in London. Knowing her reputation for honesty, they did not want to invite her to the press showing, in case she did not like the film. After the showing, Agatha walked out of the cinema and said that she thought it 'a delightful film', and it was one of the happy moments of her life, knowing that finally one of her books had been put into a film that she was delighted with.

The Times described the film as 'touchingly loyal' to Agatha Christie. *Murder on the Orient Express* was Great Britain's biggest export for the year 1974. The film was given a London premiere at the ABC Cinema in Shaftesbury Avenue in the presence of Her Majesty the Queen. This was the last public event that Agatha was well enough to attend. Although she had been taken into the theatre in a wheelchair, when it came time for the 84-year-old to be presented to the Queen, she was determined to stand, and remained standing until Princess Anne had congratulated her as well.

The film won three British Film Awards in 1975: Best Picture of the Year; Albert Finney won as the Best Film Actor; and Wendy Hiller as the Best Actress of the Year.

In America the film was nominated for six Oscars: best leading actor, best cinematography, best costume design, best music, best screenplay adaptation, but eventually it won just one – Best Supporting Actress was awarded to Ingrid Bergman who had taught herself Swedish-English for the role.

Agatha Christie was however less than satisfied with Albert Finney's moustache. She said it was much too small for Poirot, and certainly not the finest in England as Hercule Poirot had. Albert Finney had to go through two hours of make-up every morning for two months to make him as close as possible to Agatha's description of the great detective.

Only 38 years old at the time, his costume and make-up made him appear twenty years older and 30lbs heavier. He had to wear body padding to achieve the short, solid look, but by lunchtime he would be so hot that he would leave his padding in the fridge so that it was nice and cold when he put it on again. He was also given a false nose, padded cheeks, gleaming black hair and a false moustache. Unfortunately, as Finney was also starring in a West End play at the same time, his own hair couldn't be permanently tinted for the film, and so it took four shampoos every night to get rid of the black hair dye before he could go on stage.

• *THE WITNESS FOR THE PROSECUTION* •

The Witness for the Prosecution was originally written as a short story for a magazine in 1924–25. In 1933, the story was published for the first time in a short story collection in the UK, *The Hound of Death*.

In 1953, Peter Saunders mentioned that he had read the short story and thought it could be turned into an excellent play. Agatha Christie had her doubts as she didn't feel that she would be able to write a convincing courtroom drama. After months of gentle pressure, she suggested that he try to write it himself. That is exactly what he did, to prove to her that it could be done.

When the draft of Saunders' play was delivered to Christie, she phoned him within a couple of hours to say that he hadn't written it very well, but he had shown her how it could be done. Six weeks later, the play arrived on Saunder's desk, just as she had promised. Agatha had decided to change the ending of the short story for something more visually dramatic.

When *The Witness for the Prosecution* premiered in the Winter Garden Theatre in Covent Garden on 28 October 1953, it was a sell out and a triumph. It had a cast of thirty actors and two huge sets, including one that recreated the interior of the Old Bailey courtroom. The play was well received and as the final curtain dropped, the cast turned and bowed to the upper box where Agatha Christie was seated. The audience realising the implication, turned to face the box as well and gave the author a standing ovation. As the applause grew, an embarrassed Agatha stood and left the box, but as she left she whispered to Peter Saunders 'It's rather fun, isn't it?'

Usually Agatha dreaded first nights, feeling shy and uncomfortable, but not this one. She said the play was 'so well done' and outside there were jostling crowds of women waiting:

Quite the rough types you know

anxious to shake her hand and congratulate her. One of them patted her on her back and said:

Well done Dearie!

In her autobiography she said she had been 'radiantly happy' that night, made even more so by the applause of the audience. She described it as the one night at the theatre which would always stand out in her memory.

The Witness for the Prosecution ran for 468 performances in London, then crossed to Broadway in New York, where it ran for 645 performances and won the New York Drama Critic's Circle award for the best foreign play.

In 1957, after eighteen months of trying to persuade Agatha to sell the film rights, Billy Wilder scripted and directed the film version of *Witness for the Prosecution*. Sold to United Artists for £116,000, it was a record amount for any British playwright of the day, and these film rights were gifted to Agatha's daughter Rosalind. Wilder stuck faithfully to the original stage play, and decided to film it in black and white, even though colour movies were all the rage at the time.

The movie was nominated for six Academy Awards, but it failed to win any. It took a staggering $3.75 million at the box office in the first year of its release, and underlined Agatha's long-held assertion that if only her work was not so carelessly tampered with, more adaptations for the screen might be successful.

5

FAMILY AND LIFELINE

AGATHA MARY CLARISSA MILLER was born on 15 September 1890 in a large house called Ashfield, set in 2 acres of land, in Torquay, South Devon. Ashfield was one of the largest houses in Barton Road, and extensive alterations were completed before the family moved in, including the building of a large dining room where it was said 120 people could dance in comfort.

She was baptised on 20 November 1890 at All Saints' church in the parish of Tormohun, and shown on the register as daughter of Clarissa Margaret and Frederick Alvah Miller, whose rank or profession was given as 'Gentleman'.

The Millers first discovered Torquay as a holiday destination where both their American and British friends met. In her autobiography, Agatha Christie writes of her mother having had Rudyard Kipling and Henry James to tea. The Millers strove to become accepted in the upper-middle-class society of Torquay. Agatha spoke of her father's pride in making a large monetary contribution in Agatha's name to the building of a new church for Tormohun parish.

• AGATHA'S FATHER •

Her father was Frederick Alvah Miller (1846–1901), an American stockbroker with an independent income. His own father, Nathaniel, had worked his way up from clerkship to partnership in one of New York's largest companies. Therefore, Frederick, as the son of a rich man, had never trained for a trade or a profession, and attended Vevey, an exclusive preparatory school in Switzerland. As a young man, Frederick Miller had flirted with the heiress Jenny Jerome, who would later become the mother of Winston Churchill.

Moving to England from America, Mr Miller enjoyed his role as a man of leisure. Every morning he went to his club, returning by cab for lunch. In the afternoons he returned to the club to play whist, and then stayed there until it was time to return home to change for dinner. At least once a week, there was a dinner party at Ashfield, and Mr & Mrs Miller dined out several times a week.

However, the family income was gradually reducing due to failing investments and money worries meant that Mr Miller's health began to deteriorate. He died suddenly at the age of 55, whilst he was in London searching for some added means of income. His death certificate indicates the cause of death as 'complications from Bright's Disease'. His daughter Agatha was only 11 years old.

• AGATHA'S MOTHER •

Her mother, Clarissa 'Clara' Margaret Miller (*née* Boehmer) was the daughter of a British Army captain (1855–1926). On Agatha's second marriage certificate, her mother's maiden name is recorded as Beamer, perhaps indicating how the name was pronounced.

Twenty-four-year-old Clara had married 32-year-old Frederick Miller, her step-cousin, in 1878, and the two enjoyed twenty-three years of marriage. Mrs Miller was an imposing woman, with a natural elegance, dignity and flair for stylish clothes. She was without doubt the most influential person in Agatha's life.

Clara convinced her daughter that she could do anything she put her mind to. She was an unusual mother for her generation because she let Agatha run wild as much as she liked, as if she were a boy. Although both Clara and Agatha were shy women, they were not lacking in nerve. After the death of Clara's husband, Agatha was the only child at home, and so she received all her mother's attention and affection.

When Clara died in 1926, Agatha's world was to fall apart.

• AGATHA'S SIBLINGS •

Agatha was the youngest of three children. Her elder brother, Louis Montant 'Monty' Miller was ten years older (1880–1929); and her sister was Margaret Frary 'Madge' Miller, eleven years her senior (1879–1950).

Monty was educated at Harrow, but he had a troubled childhood and was expelled from Harrow for reasons unknown. By 1901 when his father died, Monty had made an unsuccessful attempt to start a career as an engineer, and when the Boer War broke out in 1899, he volunteered for the Royal Welsh Regiment. After the war he obtained a commission in the East Surrey Regiment in India.

He was said to be handsome, clever and charming, capable of fascinating women and then fleecing those who fell in love with him. His name was never mentioned before the publication of Agatha's autobiography, but it appears that according to Maida & Spornick she considered him 'amoral, difficult, destructive but most charming'. As far as Agatha was concerned, Monty left everything to be desired as an older brother, and treated his younger sister, who adored him, with indifference.

After India, he served in East Africa, but was wounded and came home critically ill. The police visited Ashfield to caution Monty who was alleged to have been involved in illegal activities in the ivory trade in Africa. He confessed to Agatha that he had led a wicked life and fallen foul of the law throughout the world:

But my word, kid ... I've had a thundering good time.

Agatha and her sister Madge provided him with a cottage in Dartmoor where he lived with a nurse-companion on funds provided by the family. Later on a trip to France, he fell seriously ill and Agatha funded his retirement to a small cottage in southern France. Monty failed to reach his 50th birthday, dying of a cerebral haemorrhage whilst in a Marseilles café in 1929. He was buried in France.

Agatha's attitude towards her brother was complicated, but in 1929, at around the time of Monty's death, she met Colonel Dywer of the King's African Rifles who had known Monty as 'Puffing Billy' Miller during the war. His testimony that Agatha's brother was 'one of the bravest chaps' he had ever known, and had impressed his comrades by being utterly fearless, despite his eccentricities, had a profound effect on Agatha's view of her brother.

Agatha's sister Madge, affectionately known as 'Punkie', grew up when there was plenty of money in the family, few worries and many advantages. She went to Roedean (then known as the Misses Lawrence's School), went to Paris for finishing school and then had her 'coming out' season in New York.

About nine months after her father's death, Madge married James Watt, the son of a prosperous textile owner in Manchester. Nan Watts, James' little sister, was a bridesmaid with Agatha at the wedding and the two became best friends for life.

Madge was a talented writer who had several short stories published in magazines, including *Vanity Fair*. In 1924 Madge's play *The Claimant*, about a great Victorian fraud, ran in the West End at the Queen's Theatre. This was to be her only success on the professional stage.

Madge and James had a little boy called Jack, and Agatha adored her nephew. Madge suffered badly from arthritis in her old age, which made visits to her sister more difficult, and she died in August 1950.

• EDUCATION AND GROWING UP •

Due to the age gap between the siblings, Agatha's elder brother and sister were away at school whilst she was growing up, and so she had to learn to entertain herself. She later attributed her furtive imagination to a lonely and bored childhood. However, she also claimed to be totally happy in her own company and as Gwen Robyns said: 'with imagination, a simple hoop could be turned into an engine, a glorious white stallion or a sea monster'.

Agatha never went to school and was educated at home by her mother and occasional part-time tutors. This was characteristic of the period when mainly only boys went to school, although Agatha's mother, who was not one to follow convention, had sent her elder sister Madge to school. At that time, her mother believed that children should get the best education. But, when the time came for Agatha to go to school, her mother's views had changed. She now believed passionately that education destroyed a child's brains and ruined the eyesight.

Agatha's mother had intended that Agatha should be able to read by the age of 8, but by 5 Agatha had already taught herself. Her mother encouraged her to write poetry and short stories – she had some of these poems published in *The Poetry Review*, but was less successful in getting her short stories published. Mr Miller had started teaching her elementary mathematics and soon discovered that she had a natural mathematical brain. Mrs Miller taught her history and general knowledge, and insisted that Agatha read newspaper articles as they were essential to a developing mind.

Agatha's second husband Max was of the view that if she had been sent to school, the effect would have been harmful to her wonderful natural imagination. After Mr Miller died, Agatha was taken to arithmetic classes twice a week. There were also piano, singing and dancing lessons, as music was the one area in which Agatha was always taught professionally.

Before her father's death, Agatha had a loving yet distant relationship with her parents, since upper-middle-class children living in large houses with servants did not usually see a great deal of their parents. Agatha's parents also travelled frequently for pleasure or for their health, leaving their children behind, and this was also a theme for both Agatha and Madge with their children. Shortly after the birth of her daughter, for example, Agatha and her husband went on a round-the-world trip, leaving Rosalind behind in Madge's care.

A local friend of the family, Eden Phillpott (the renowned West Country author) encouraged Agatha's writing, and presented one of Agatha's first manuscripts, entitled 'Snow upon the Desert', to his literary agent in London but, unfortunately, without success.

At the age of 16, Agatha was sent to finishing school in Paris for two years, where she studied singing and piano – her first formal education. Paris at the time was filled with small well-established finishing schools run by sisters of a convent or formidable *mademoiselles*. Agatha was an accomplished pianist but shyness and stage fright prevented her pursuing a career in music. In Paris, Agatha combined a musical training with visits to art galleries and instruction in painting. Enforced visits to the Louvre resulted in an aversion to the Old Masters which, according to Max, took many years to overcome.

After finishing school in Paris, Agatha spent three months in Egypt with her mother in 1910. Clara had become restless without her husband, and after suffering a number of minor heart attacks since his death, she had begun to travel, often taking Agatha with her, and so starting Agatha Christie's life-long love of travel.

For Agatha, Cairo provided an opportunity to 'come out' among the army officers at reduced cost. Rounds of parties and dances deliberately threw well-chaperoned young ladies and gentlemen together to encourage them to contract suitable engagements within their own upper-class circles.

Agatha, who in later life was to become absorbed by archaeology, was not at the time in the slightest bit interested in the antiquities of Egypt. She was quite open about the skill she acquired in Cairo – she learnt to flirt. She said that a girl's duty was 'to listen with every appearance of awestruck admiration'. To her admirers, she seemed timelessly English. She was, without having to think about it, a lady.

• ENGAGEMENT AND MARRIAGE •

Agatha, with an oval face, fair hair and blue eyes, was confident about her good looks as a young woman. She enjoyed being a young woman in an age when young men were easily carried away into marriage proposals, of which Agatha appears to have received nine. Agatha fell hopelessly and silently in love twice with tall young men who could not afford to propose to her.

She had three 'understandings' or engagements: one with a man fifteen years older who wrote beautiful love letters, but when they met had nothing to say; and one with a naval lieutenant with whom she had plenty to talk about, until he became fascinated and obsessed by theosophy and spiritualist mediums. The third was the older brother of her friends the Lucy girls. Reggie was an army major in the Gunners, 'gentle and unhurried', but his lack of romance and jealousy left her dissatisfied.

In 1912 Agatha, officially engaged to Reggie Lucy, met and fell in love with Lieutenant Archibald Christie of the Royal Field Artillery, who was stationed in Exeter. It is quite clear that from the moment she saw him Agatha was swept off her feet, whilst Archie was fascinated by the vivacious girl he had met.

Archie Christie proposed to Agatha after attending a Wagner concert performed at the Torquay Pavilion in January 1913, now sadly converted into a shopping centre.

Agatha Christie Mile – which takes in the landmarks associated with Agatha's life in Torquay.

Archie was described as 'good and steady, very popular and one of the better types', by his commander. Agatha's second husband described him as 'a masterful airman of great charm and determination, a man who never failed to get his way'. Agatha's mother was less influenced by Archie's charm, instead seeing a certain ruthlessness of character, and she feared for her vulnerable daughter.

Agatha accepted a proposal of marriage from Archie after attending a Wagner concert performed by the Torquay Municipal Orchestra at the Pavilion in January 1913, just three months after they had met.

After a two-year tempestuous engagement, Agatha and Archibald were married at short notice and by special license at the parish church of Emmanuel, Clifton, Bristol, on Christmas Eve 1914. There is no doubt from her autobiography that Agatha would have preferred to wait. Agatha, then aged 24, was married in a coat, skirt and purple velvet hat and did not even have time to wash her hands or face.

They caught the train to Torquay, arriving at midnight and crossed the road from the station to the Grand Hotel, where they had a one-day honeymoon.

Archie, who by now was one of the first pilots in the Royal Flying Corps, returned to his unit just two days later, on Boxing Day 1914. Agatha returned to live with her mother at Ashfield, and continued to live there until 1918, reunited with Archie only for rare, brief and rapturous reunions.

Agatha and Archie
spent their one-night
honeymoon at the Grand
Hotel, Torquay.

According to some reports, they spent only six days together
in their first year of marriage.

When Torquay Town Hall was turned into a hospital,
Agatha Christie had a chance to fulfil a childhood ambition
of becoming a nurse. She worked as a VAD (Volunteer Aid
Detachment), nursing casualties of the war. Agatha was an
excellent nurse, and given different circumstances, would
have been happy to have worked as a professional nurse.

After two years nursing casualties, Christie went to work
in the dispensary, where she relished the responsibility and
learnt basic chemistry and knowledge of medicines, herbs and
poisons, as well as taking the examination to become accred-
ited by the Society of Apothecaries.

Meanwhile, Archie was mentioned four times in dispatches, and rose to the rank of colonel in the Royal Flying Corps, later to become the Royal Air Force. Colonel Christie was awarded the Distinguished Service Order, the Order of St Stanislaus Third Class with swords, and became a Companion of St Michael and St George.

Archie was a typical Englishman and tried to laugh off the traumatic experiences of front-line combat, refusing to talk about the war on his short periods at home. Agatha on the other hand felt that her nursing experiences were making her more serious. Unconsciously they were growing in different directions, with Agatha feeling herself to have become more sensible, and Archie more frivolous. Archie wanted a wife who was carefree and beautiful, untroubled by the worries of the world, but Agatha was disheartened by Archie's refusal to recognise the good work she was doing for the war efforts.

After the war, Archie was posted to the Air Ministry, and they had to move away from Devon to a small flat in London.

• AGATHA'S FIRST NOVEL •

Agatha Christie had been toying with the idea of writing a detective novel for a while, although it is claimed that her sister told her she was incapable! Her new knowledge of poisons and the desire to prove her sister wrong inspired her to start at the age of 25. Having completed half of the book however, Agatha got writer's block and so the family suggested she take herself off to a remote Dartmoor hotel to finish the novel. In the peace and quiet of Dartmoor during the summer of 1916, *The Mysterious Affair at Styles* was finished within a fortnight.

Archie Christie recommended that the manuscript be sent to a friend who was a director at the publishers, Methuen. After six months' wait, Methuen rejected it. Another publisher was approached, with exactly the same result.

Finally, the manuscript was submitted to Bodley Head. After a delay of nearly two years, Bodley Head accepted the book, but suggested an alternative final chapter and other changes. They also required her to sign a very tough contract which saw Agatha earn hardly any money for her first, or indeed her next four, novels. *The Mysterious Affair at Styles* was published in 1920.

• AGATHA'S DAUGHTER •

Very soon after the end of the First World War, Agatha found herself pregnant. Archie desperately wanted a girl, fearing a boy would make him jealous.

Agatha's only child, a daughter called Rosalind Margaret Clarissa Christie, was born at Ashfield on 5 August 1919. Agatha was aged 28, and she and Archie had been married five years. Weighing in at 8.5lbs, Rosalind was born with thick black hair. As she grew up, Agatha describes her variously as very bright, beautiful, energetic, outgoing and strong-minded.

Agatha and Archie moved back out of London to Sunningdale in Berkshire, where, after living in a mansion flat, they bought a house in 1924 and named it Styles after Christie's first novel.

Rosalind was educated at boarding school, first Caledonia School in Bexhill, Sussex at the age of 9, and then on to the exclusive private school Benenden. She went to finishing schools in Switzerland and Paris, and also stayed in Germany before her debutante season in London.

Once her parents had separated, she continued to see her father and wrote to him regularly, but she did complain that on a Sunday evening at boarding school she had to write two letters home to her parents, whereas all the other girls only had to write one.

She also got on well with her stepfather Max, but it wasn't until she accompanied them both on an archaeological dig that she realised how hard he worked. Until then, according to Janet Morgan, she had thought his life consisted of 'writing, reading, and good meals'.

Rosalind became engaged to Hubert Prichard, an officer in the Royal Welch Fusiliers, whose home was Pwllywrach in the Vale of Glamorgan in Wales. Twelve years Rosalind's senior, they were married in June 1940 when Rosalind was 20 years old.

The relationship between mother and daughter has rarely been discussed, but it is interesting to note that Rosalind only told her mother a few days in advance that she was going to marry Hubert Prichard. She said that she was only letting

Agatha know because Hubert had insisted on it. Rosalind's apparent reluctance to include Agatha in the wedding has been seen as part independence and part reluctance to be overshadowed by her famous mother.

On 21 September 1943 their son Mathew, Agatha's only grandchild, was born. Hubert was stationed in France when the child was born and was only able to visit the baby once before he was killed in action in 1944.

Agatha spent a considerable amount of time in Wales with her daughter and grandson, helping Rosalind to cope with a small baby in an unheated house with no staff. Agatha admired her daughter's courage and stamina, but felt unable to give her the emotional support she needed. In her autobiography however she wrote that one of the hardest and saddest things in life is to watch someone you love suffering from grief. Agatha decided that the best thing she could do was to carry on as usual and say as little as possible.

Agatha was delighted when, in October 1949, Rosalind announced that she was marrying Anthony Hicks. Although trained as a barrister and called to the Bar, Anthony had decided that it was not right for him as he did not have the rapid mental agility so necessary in court.

Max said that Anthony was 'the kindest man he had ever known and that he would literally would not hurt a fly'. A born scholar and a man with profound and wide interests, at the time of his marriage to Rosalind he was reading Tibetan as well as Sanskrit at the School of Oriental and African Studies.

Eventually, he turned his attention to horticulture, and when they moved into Agatha's house in 1968, he benefited Greenway not only by his knowledge of plants but through a natural flair for the economics of the business.

• 1926 – AN ANNUS HORRIBILIS •

In 1926 Agatha's mother died of bronchitis. Shortly afterwards, Agatha moved into her mother's home at Ashfield to clear out the house, leaving Archie by himself. Archie arrived at Ashfield for Rosalind's birthday, and announced to his wife that he had fallen in love with another woman and wanted a divorce.

The Christies had been slowly drifting apart, spending less and less time together. One of the key reasons for this was the game of golf which caused a complete separation of interest. When Agatha first brought her husband to the Purley Downs Golf Club in South Croydon in 1923 and introduced him to the game, it had been with the intention of spending time together. The weekend was *theirs*. She always made a point of storing her notebooks and typewriter away at the weekend, to devote herself to the man she loved. However, over time, Archie became obsessed with golf and started to spend his weekends away from Agatha, absorbed in the game and his new friends.

The Christies' marriage was no longer providing the mutual support that it once had. When Archie became depressed at not being able to get a job following their return from the round-the-world trip, he suggested that Agatha should go and spend more time with her mother and sister because she never seemed to be grave or gay at the right times for him.

When Clara died, Archie was no help to Agatha emotionally, as he wanted a wife who was good humoured and high spirited, and he urged her to buck herself up. Instead, Agatha went to Ashfield and locked herself away in the misery of her bereavement. She neglected her husband, and understandably withdrew into herself and mourned her mother.

Although Archie had for some time been dropping hints that Agatha was losing the youthful looks that had originally attracted him, it never occurred to Agatha that her loyal and honourable husband of eleven years, who was devoted to their daughter, would find a more suitable companion.

The more suitable companion was a 25-year-old secretary, Nancy Neele, of Croxley Green, near Rickmansworth, who was ten years younger than Archie. She had been a friend of a friend, and as well as becoming Archie's regular golfing partner, she had also been a house guest of Agatha and Archie's at their home, Styles.

In the midst of her grief, Archie broke the news to Agatha that he had fallen in love with Nancy and there was no going back. The news came to Agatha as a completely unexpected and shattering blow, never even remotely suspected.

Archie had been expecting his wife to be unhappy, but he did not expect the vehement opposition to a divorce that he got. She could not accept that he no longer loved her, or that he would abandon Rosalind and herself to marry another woman. She refused to give him a divorce. Archie continued to see Nancy on weekends at the homes of understanding friends, and it is said that he applied increasingly brutal pressure on Agatha to agree to divorce.

The shock proved too much for Agatha and she gave way to complete despair.

• THE DISAPPEARANCE •

Agatha Christie disappeared for eleven days on 3 December 1926. Around 9.45 p.m., she went upstairs to kiss her sleeping daughter, Rosalind, and then left the house. Archie was staying for the weekend at a house party given by Mr & Mrs F. James at Hurstmore Cottage, Godalming, where Miss Neele had also been invited. There were just the four of them, no other guests.

Agatha Christie's Morris Cowley car was found abandoned on a slope in Newlands Corner, near Guilford, Surrey. There was no sign of her. For eleven days the country was fascinated by her disappearance and a nationwide manhunt got underway.

Agatha was eventually found staying at a hotel in Harrogate (the Swan Hydropathic Hotel, now called the Old Swan Hotel) under the name of Mrs Teresa Neele of Cape Town. However, Agatha Christie's discovery in such strange circumstances raised more questions than answers.

According to the hotel manager, Agatha arrived by taxi on Saturday morning with only a small suitcase and was given room 105 on the first floor with hot and cold water. She signed the register Teresa Neele, Cape Town, South Africa.

Agatha claimed that she suffered amnesia after a nervous breakdown, following the death of her mother and the end of her marriage. On 16 February 1928, Agatha gave a full account to the *Daily Mail* of the events leading up to and including her disappearance in 1926, or at least as far as she could recall them. This was the last time she ever discussed it. Agatha Christie never made any mention of this event afterwards, not even in her autobiography. Her daughter said in the 1980s that her mother did not mention the disappearance as she had no memory of it. Even her second husband Max's memoirs, published two years after Agatha's death, made barely any mention of the disappearance. The family closed ranks.

Some commentators, such as G.C. Ramsey, believe that the amnesia has since been verified beyond any shadow of doubt as genuine. Other commentators at the time felt that it had all been a publicity stunt and they condemned Agatha for setting off such an expensive public search. Questions were asked in parliament about the expenditure of public money in the search for the famous detective writer, which had made front-page news for days.

The third school of thought was that Mrs Christie knew exactly what she as doing – she decided to teach her husband a lesson, never dreaming that the press would get hold of the story, intending instead that it would remain a private incident. Once it became a worldwide story, all she could do was sit tight until she was found and stick to her story of amnesia. In 1999 author Jared Cade published a fascinating book revealing that Nan Watts' daughter and son-in-law had confirmed the 'teaching the husband a lesson' story. The disappearance, Cade claimed, had all been planned with Agatha's best friend Nan's cooperation.

The most interesting repercussions was that by registering at the Harrogate Hydropathic under the name of Neele, Agatha Christie successfully put the name of the 'other woman' on the front page of every newspaper. Her husband had tried desperately to keep Nancy's name out of the divorce courts and the press.

Nancy Neele's father was hounded by the press and eventually issued a statement, in an effort to salvage the family's reputation, expressing consternation over the involvement of his daughter. He said he could not understand why Mrs Christie would use his family's name. He told them that there was not the slightest reason for associating Nancy with the disappearance of Mrs Christie. He claimed his daughter has been a friend of both Colonel and Mrs Christie for some time, but had never been especially friends with the Colonel. Shortly after this statement was made, Nancy was sent off by her parents, Charles and Mable Neele, on an round-the-world cruise.

The effect of Agatha Christie's disappearance on the sales of her books was highly beneficial over the next three years, and increased her fame worldwide. According to Elizabeth Walker who was the editor at Collins Publishers, *The Murder of Roger Ackroyd* (1926) which was published prior to the disappearance, sold about 4,000 copies.

Following her disappearance however, the effect of press publicity on her next book *The Big Four* (1927) was apparent, and it sold over double that of previous books, at about 8,500 copies. The next two books, *The Mystery of the Blue Train* and *The Seven Dials Mystery* sold 7,000 and 8,000 copies respectively.

James Watts, Agatha's brother-in-law, proved solidly reliable and convinced Agatha to believe what her secretary and friend Carlotta had always said, that there was no possibility of Archie ever coming back to her.

Agatha finally agreed to a divorce, even though in the 1920s divorce was still considered distasteful and taboo. The settlement was that Agatha should not cite Nancy as the third party in the divorce, in return for the custody of Rosalind. Archie made it clear that if she did not comply, he would tell the court that she had disappeared as a publicity stunt. Terrified of further notoriety, she agreed not to contest the evidence that the grounds were adultery with an unknown woman in a London hotel and Miss Nancy Neele was in no way involved.

Archie and Agatha Christie's divorce was finalised on 29 October 1928. He married Nancy Neele just over two weeks later, on 16 November in a private ceremony at

St George's Church, in Hanover Square, London. They lived happily until their deaths over thirty years later. Nancy Christie died of cancer in 1958 and Archie Christie died four years later in December 1962. They had one son, Archibald Christie III.

Ironically Mathew Prichard, Archie's grandson, had only recently attempted to get back in touch with his grandfather, writing to him from Eton about the possibility of meeting. Archie was excited about finally getting to see his grandson after nearly twenty years, and although dates were arranged, Archie died just a few days before they were due to meet.

The divorce was a traumatic time for Agatha, and she even wrote to her publisher requesting that all future books should be published with a change of name. However, the publishers felt that Agatha Christie was a name that the public had now got used to, and it was too valuable a trademark to give up. In her autobiography, she says that this was the time when she finally accepted that she was a writer, that this was her profession, and that by writing she could earn the money she needed to support herself and her child.

• A Second Marriage •

In 1930 Agatha Christie visited Baghdad for a second time, to see the archaeological dig at Ur. It was here that she met Max Edgar Lucien Mallowan, an archaeologist who was fourteen years her junior. Agatha saw that Max was one of the most obliging people at the dig, easy going and capable of handling even the temperamental wife of the lead archaeologist, Katharine Woolley. Max was quiet and serious but showed great talent for archaeological field work. As a fluent speaker of many modern languages, Max picked up Arabic fast, and impressed Agatha with his excellent handling of the native labourers.

It was suggested by the Woolleys that Max should take Agatha on a round trip to Baghdad to see something of the desert and places of interest on the journey. It was an adventurous journey, and at the end of it, Agatha felt that Max was amongst her dearest friends. As a result, she invited him to Ashfield for a holiday of picnics and walks on Dartmoor.

One night he astonished Agatha by coming to her room to return a book, and telling her that he wanted to marry her. She said it had never occurred to her that they would be anything other than friends. She objected on grounds of their fourteen-year age gap and because of his religion, as he was Catholic, and the Catholic Church would refuse to recognise his marriage to a divorcee.

However, Agatha soon realised 'that nothing in the world would be as delightful as being married to Max'. Her sister objected strongly on grounds of age, and this caused Agatha to worry all over again when she discovered that Max had been up to Oxford at the same time as her nephew Jack, whom she had cradled in her arms as a teenager.

Only her daughter Rosalind seemed pragmatic about the general idea of her mother remarrying, and declared herself happy with the choice of Max as someone who might well prove useful for sailing and tennis. However, the 11-year-old earnestly asked her mother if she realised that she would now have to share a bed with Max. Agatha assured her daughter that the fact had not escaped her!

On 11 September 1930 Agatha Christie married Max Mallowan quietly in St Cuthbert's church in the St Giles district of Edinburgh, to avoid the publicity which may have accompanied a wedding in London. Rosalind was a witness. (In her autobiography, Agatha incorrectly states that she married at St Columba's church.) In accordance with Scottish marriage laws, Agatha had spent just over two weeks holidaying on the Isle of Skye, while the banns were read, and where no reporter would ever hear them!

Agatha Christie became Agatha Christie Mallowan, although she preferred to be known amongst friends and acquaintances as Mrs Mallowan. They were to stay married for forty-six years, until her death in 1976.

Theirs appears to have been a happy marriage. Max said that 'few men are lucky enough to know what it is to live in harmony beside an imaginative, creative mind which inspires life with zest'. In his memoirs, Max said that having quarrelsome parents, bred in him a determination to make a success of marriage by inclining his temperament towards peaceful companionship, and a real feeling of regret when he himself had been quarrelsome.

A.L. Rowse remembers that Max and Agatha attended one of his lectures to the Royal Society of Literature about the sex life of the Elizabethans. Agatha apparently commented afterwards to Rowse that she did hope the lecture wouldn't start up Max again!

Jared Cade's claims that Max spent many years having a relationship with his assistant Barbara Parker, whom he then married in September 1977, just eighteen months after Agatha's death, don't appear to have been substantiated by any other source. Rosalind was certainly not particularly happy with the union, preferring that Max should have remained a 'faithful and mourning widower' according to Richard Hack.

Sir Max, knighted in 1968, was one of Britain's most distinguished archaeologists and the author of several books on his excavation work. He was a Fellow of All Souls, Oxford, a professor emeritus of western Asiatic archaeology in the University of London, and a trustee of the British Museum.

• LATER LIFE •

The 1930s were one of Agatha Christie's most prolific times for producing novels: fourteen Hercule Poirot novels, two Jane Marple novels, two Superintendent Battle books, a book of stories featuring Harley Quin and another featuring Mr Parker Pyne, four non-series mystery novels, one Mary Westmacott novel and two original plays. Max was supportive and encouraged her in her writing.

The yearly routine of journeying to the desert in the late autumn for six months of archaeological digs, of summers in

Devon, Christmas with her sister's family at Abney, and stays in London and Wallingford, provided a delightful life. Max and Agatha enjoyed being together, and wrote constantly to each other when they were apart. Their lack of children was a sadness, as Agatha miscarried in the first year or two of their marriage, but apart from this, the Mallowans formed a pattern of marital life that most would envy.

Agatha Christie accompanied her husband on his archaeological expeditions for nearly twenty years, and her book *Come, Tell Me How You Live* describes her days on the archaeological digs in Syria. She describes her struggle trying to buy suitable sensible lightweight dresses, in regrettably large sizes, and her role as both excavation photographer and archaeological assistant, with her own unique technique for cleaning precious artefacts using face cream.

During the Second World War (1939–45), after an unsatisfactory period with the Home Guard, Max got a commission in the RAF Volunteer Reserve, and work in the Air Ministry, ending up in Cairo. After renewing her training as a dispenser, Agatha worked part time in London's University College Hospital's dispensary. For about three years, she put in regular hours of two full days, three half days, and Saturday mornings each week, and filled in when other workers were unable to get to the hospital.

She said in an interview with the *Sunday Times* that there was little else to do in the evenings during the war, except write, and as a result she was able to produce twelve complete novels.

It was during the Second World War that Agatha Christie wrote the two novels *Curtain* and *Sleeping Murder*, which were intended as the last cases of her two great detectives, Hercule Poirot and Jane Marple, respectively. Both books were sealed in a bank vault for over thirty years, with *Curtain* being released for publication towards the end of her life, and *Sleeping Murder* posthumously.

Max returned six months after the end of the war and Agatha, who had not been expecting him, had arrived minutes earlier from a visit to Rosalind in Wales. Agatha had been nervous about seeing Max, concerned that she had grown fat, but she needn't have worried. Max had also put on weight and he couldn't have cared less about her size.

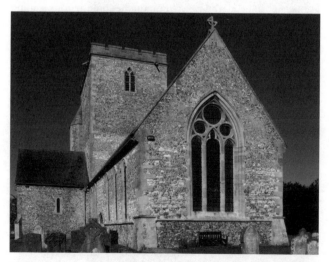

St Mary's church in Cholsey, Oxfordshire, where Agatha Christie is buried

In July 1971, whilst in London, Agatha fell and broke her hip but, believing it just to be bruised, she hobbled round for a week in great pain. Though the leg was to mend, many said that she never quite recovered, and her health began to deteriorate.

Agatha Christie died peacefully on 12 January 1976, aged 85, of natural causes at her home in Wallingford, Oxfordshire. After a private ceremony, she was buried in St Mary's church-yard in Cholsey, Oxfordshire.

Agatha's gravestone was just as she had planned it in St Mary's churchyard, Cholsey, Oxfordshire.

Her gravestone was just as she had planned it, with lines from Spenser's *Faerie Queene*:

In Memorium

Agatha Mary Clarissa Christie

Mallowan

DBE

Agatha Christie - Author & Playwright

Born 15th Sept 1890 - Died 12th Jan 1976

Sleep after toyle, port after stormie seas

Ease after warre, death after life doth greatly please

· BIBLIOGRAPHY ·

Bargainnier, Earl F., *The Gentle Art of Murder*, 1980

Barnard, Robert, *A Talent to Deceive*, 1980

Cade, Jared, *Agatha Christie and the Eleven Missing Days*, 1998

Campbell, Mark, *The Pocket Essential Agatha Christie*, 2005

Christie, Agatha, *Autobiography*, 1977

Craig, Patricia & Cadogan, Mary, *The Lady Investigates, Women Detectives & Spies in Fiction*, 1981

Curran, John, *Agatha Christie's Murder in the Making*, 2011

Curran, John, *Agatha Christie's Secret Notebooks*, 2009

Fido, Martin, *The World of Agatha Christie* 1999

Fienman, Jeffery, *The Mysterious World of Agatha Christie*, 1975

Fitzgibbon, Russell H., *The Agatha Christie Companion*, 1980

Gerald, Michael C., *The Poisonous Pen of Agatha Christie*, 1993

Gill, Gillian, *Agatha Christie: The Woman and her Mysteries*, 1990

Gregg, Hubert, *Agatha Christie and all that Mousetrap*, 1980

Hack, Richard, *The Duchess of Death*, 2009

Haining, Peter, *Agatha Christie Murder in Four Acts*, 1990

Hart, Anne, *The Life and Times of Hercule Poirot*, 1990

Hart, Anne, *The Life and Times of Miss Jane Marple*, 1997

Hawthorne, Bret, *Agatha Christie's Devon*, 2009

Haycroft, Howard, *Murder for Pleasure*, 1942

Holgate, Mike, *Stranger than Fiction, Agatha Christie's True Crime Inspirations* 2010

Keating, H.R.F., *Agatha Christie First Lady of Crime*, 1977

Macaskill, Hilary, *Agatha Christie at Home*, 2009

Maida, Prof. Patricia D. & Spornick, Prof. Nicholas B., *Murder She Wrote, A Study of Agatha Christie's Detective Fiction*, 1982

Mallowan, Agatha Christie, *Come Tell Me How You Live*, 1946

Mallowan, Max, *Mallowan's Memoirs*, 1977

McCall, Henrietta, *The Life of Max Mallowan*, 2001

Morgan, Janet, *Agatha Christie A Biography*, 1984

Murdoch, Derrick, *The Agatha Christie Mystery*, 1976

Norman, Dr Andrew, *Agatha Christie: The Finished Portrait*, 2006

Osborne, Charles, *The Life and Crimes of Agatha Christie*, 1982

Ramsey, G.C., *Agatha Christie: Mistress of Mystery*, 1967

Riley & McAllister, *The Bedside, Bathtub & Armchair Companion to Agatha Christie*, 1979

Robyns, Gwen, *The Mystery of Agatha Christie*, 1978

Rowland, Susan, *From Agatha Christie to Ruth Rendell, British Women Writers in Detective and Crime Fiction*, 2001

Rowse, A.L., *Memories and Glimpses*, 1986

Sanders, Dennis & Lovallo, Len, *The Agatha Christie Companion*, 1984

Sova, Dawn B., *Agatha Christie A to Z*, 1996

Symons, Julian, *The Detective Story in Britain*, 1962

The Agatha Christie Collection Magazines

Thomspon, Laura, *Agatha Christie*, 2007

Toye, Randall, *The Agatha Christie Who's Who*, 1988

Underwood, Lynn, *Agatha Christie Official Centenary Celebration*, 1990

Wynne, Nancy Blu, *An Agatha Christie Chronology*, 1976

Also available in this series:

"How often have I said
to you that when you
have eliminated the
impossible, whatever
remains, however
improbable, must be the
truth?" *The Sign of Four*

THE

Sherlock Holmes

MISCELLANY

ROGER JOHNSON
& JEAN UPTON

FOREWORD BY GYLES BRANDRETH

978 0 7524 7152 5

Visit our website and discover thousands of
other History Press books.

www.thehistorypress.co.uk

Also available in this series:

"It is a truth universally acknowledged, that a single man in possession of a good fortune must be in want of a wife."
Pride and Prejudice

THE

Jane Austen

MISCELLANY

LAUREN NIXON

978 0 7524 6863 1

Visit our website and discover thousands of other History Press books.

www.thehistorypress.co.uk